ENGLISH G

LIGHTHOUSE
Workbook
5

Vokabeltrainer-App
Verfügbar für: iOS, Android und Windows Phone

Deine interaktiven Übungen findest du hier:

1. Melde dich auf scook.de an.
2. Gib den unten stehenden Zugangscode in die Box ein.
3. Hab viel Spaß mit deinen interaktiven Übungen.

Dein Zugangscode auf
www.scook.de

Die interaktiven Übungen können dort nach Bestätigung der allgemeinen Geschäftsbedingungen genutzt werden.

uqcrx-zskuh

INHALT

UNIT 1	Life down under	4
UNIT 2	Respect	19
UNIT 3	Looking forward	33
UNIT 4	Generation *like*	40

EXAM PREPARATION	61
SAMPLE ANSWERS	69
DIFF BANK	71
REVISION Lösungen	83
PARTNER B	84
LANGUAGE FILE kompakt	85

So viele Zeichen im Workbook – was bedeuten sie?

Die Ampel – Wie schwer fällt dir eine Übung?
In der Ampel kannst du markieren, wie schwer dir eine (Teil-)Übung gefallen ist.
rot = schwer, gelb = mittel, grün = leicht.

Leere und volle Kreise – jeder so gut er kann
Leichtere Aufgaben sind mit einem leeren Kreis markiert und schwierigere mit einem vollen. Die Übungen ohne spezielle Markierungen sind auf einem Niveau, das alle Schülerinnen und Schüler lösen können.

Hören von der CD und interaktive Übungen
Die Zahl unter dem Kopfhörer nennt dir die Track-Nummer, unter der du den entsprechenden Hörtext auf der Audio-CD findest.
Das Tablet weist auf Online-Aufgabenpakete hin, die dir viele passende, interaktive Übungen anbieten. Geh auf www.scook.de, gib deinen Zugangscode ein und wähle aus dem Inhaltsverzeichnis die passende Übungszahl.

Stift und Partnerarbeit
Für Aufgaben, neben denen ein Stift abgebildet ist, schreibst du deine Antwort auf ein anderes Blatt Papier. Die verschiedenen Köpfe beziehen sich auf Partner- oder Gruppenarbeit.

Unit 1 — Life down under

1 The big Australia quiz

a) How much do you know about Australia? Tick (✓) the right answers.

1. This famous bridge goes over the harbour in …
   A Brisbane ☐ **B** Perth ☐ **C** Sydney. ✓

2. Australia's population is around …
   A 23 million ✓ **B** 44 million ☐ **C** 79 million. ☐

3. Australia's unofficial national animal is …
   A the kangaroo ✓ **B** the tiger ☐ **C** the sheep. ☐

4. Which of these is the Australian flag?
   A ☐ **B** ☐ **C** ✓

> ❗ Don't worry if you don't understand every word.
> • Some words are like German words, e.g. *kangaroo*.
> • You can guess some words from the context.

5. What is the capital of Australia?
   A Sydney ☐ **B** Canberra ✓ **C** Melbourne. ☐

6. The official colours of Australian sports teams are …
   A red and blue ☐ **B** red and gold ☐ **C** green and gold. ✓

7. Australia uses … **A** the euro ☐ **B** the Australian dollar ✓
   C the Australian pound. ☐

8. What is the large island to the south of Australia?
   A Fiji ☐
   B Tasmania ✓
   C New Zealand. ☐

   Australian-born Jacqueline Freney won eight gold medals for swimming at the London Paralympics in 2012.

9. The ocean which is NOT near Australia is …
   A the Pacific Ocean ☐ **B** the Atlantic Ocean ✓ **C** the Indian Ocean. ☐

10. What are lots of Australians especially crazy about?
    A Sport! ✓ **B** Sport! ✓ **C** Sport! ✓

🎧 **b)** Now listen and check your answers. How many did you get right?

▶ SB p. 9

THEMES 1

2 New words

a) ⭘ Match the words with their meanings. Write the letters. Look in your book on pages 195–66 if you need help.

This exercise will help you to learn these new words from Theme 1.

1. [f] continues
2. [c] best-known
3. [d] spot
4. [b] large
5. [g] sting
6. [i] exam
7. [a] as
8. [e] experts
9. [h] such as
10. [j] deadly

a because
b big
c most-famous
d place
e people who know a lot about a subject
f goes on
g bees do it
h for example
i important test
j so dangerous it can kill

▶ SB p. 11

b) ⭘ Find a different way to say the same thing in English: [More help p. 71]

1. Smoking is **banned** in restaurants. _Smoking isn't allowed_ in restaurants.
2. **Central** Australia is flat. _The middle of Australia_ is flat.
3. **One in ten** visitors is from China. – _10% of visitors are from China_.
4. Native animals will **suffer**. Life will _get worse_ for native animals.
5. It's **surprising** that bees are so dangerous. _I'm surprised that_ bees are so dangerous.

▶ SB p. 11

3 READING Info on Oz

Find the answers to questions 1–5 in the texts in Theme 1. The tip will help you.

To find information in texts:
- *First use titles and pictures and skim read to find the right place.*
- *Then read carefully to find the information.*

1. What is Australia's most dangerous animal?
   - Answer _jellyfish_   [title: "deadliest animals"; skim: "dangerous" "list" etc.]
   - Which text (A–E)? _E_

2. Are people paid to help the Rural Fire Service?
   - Answer _No, they're volunteers._   • Which text (A–E)? _C_

3. What percent (%) of people who live in Australia are immigrants?
   - Answer _25%_   • Which text (A–E)? _B_

4. What animals were brought to Australia in the 1800s and how many are there now?
   - Answer _camels – more than a million_   • Which text (A–E)? _D_

5. Why do most tourists want to see Uluru in the morning or evening?
   - Answer _It changes colour and becomes burning red._   • Which text (A–E)? _A_   ▶ SB p. 11

five 5

1 THEMES

4 Safety advice for tourists More help p. 71
Complete the article. Find words that fit the context.
Sometimes more than one word will fit.

> ! Interaktive Übungen zu dieser Seite kannst du auf www.scook.de gratis freischalten. Deinen Code findest du auf Seite 1.

In hot weather

Parts of Australia have a very hot _climate_. If you suffer from _heat_ stress you should stay in the shade and use wet towels to _cool_ down. You should also drink a lot of water, and _call/phone/see_ a doctor if you don't get better.

At the beach

Be careful if there are jellyfish[1] – bluebottles[2] are the _deadliest_. Swim with _care_ where there are strong currents[3]. And _protect_ yourself from the sun: use good suncream and _wear/take_ a hat and T-shirt.

In the outback

Take lots of _water_ with you – 10 litres per person per day. If your car breaks _down_, stay with it and use it for _shade_. If you get lost, _light/make_ a small fire and _blow/use_ your whistle.

Snakes

If a snake _bites_ you, stay calm and _still_. Phone for an ambulance and try to _identify_ the snake so the doctor can give you the right anti-venom.

▶ SB p. 13

5 SPEAKING What should I do?
How well does your partner know the advice in exercise 4?
Ask for advice for something. Your partner answers with his/her book closed! Then swap roles.

> I've been bitten by a snake!

> I'm suffering from heat stress.

> I'm going to the beach.

> I'm going to the outback.

▶ SB p. 13

6 MEDIATION One word, two meanings
Can you explain this story to your partner in German?

a bluebottle (Aus)

A woman from England was swimming at a beach in Australia. A man shouted to her: "Be very, very careful – there are bluebottles here!" The woman was surprised.
Five minutes later, a girl shouted the same thing. "How strange!" thought the woman. "These Aussies are crazy – why should I be afraid of a little fly?!"

a bluebottle (UK)

▶ SB p. 13

[1] jellyfish _Qualle_   [2] bluebottle _Portugiesische Galeere (eine Qualle)_   [3] current _Strömung_

THEMES

7 European settlers and Aboriginal Australians
Which people are described? Draw lines.

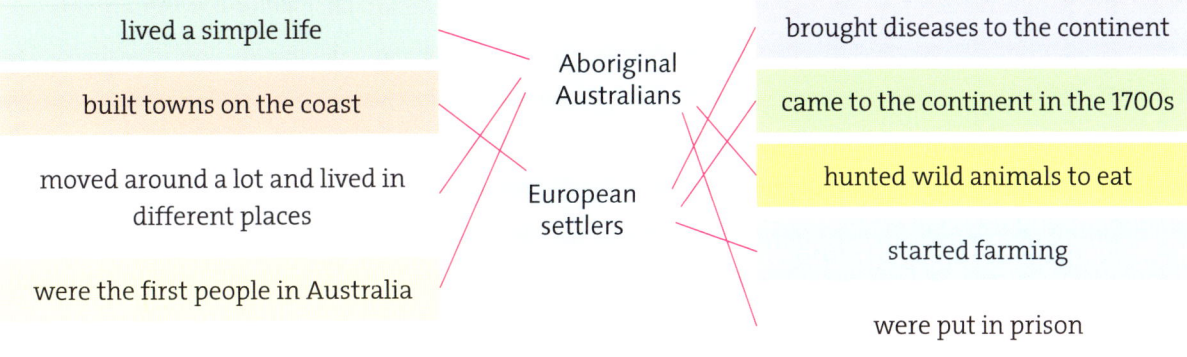

▶ SB p. 15

8 Describing a picture
Look at this dot painting by an Aboriginal artist. It's called *Aboriginal History (Facts)*.
What story do the pictures tell?
What is happening in the pictures?
Write in your exercise book. You can use a dictionary if you need to.

> at the top / bottom • on the left / right • in the middle •
> in the foreground / background • Aboriginal Australians are …-ing. •
> European settlers are …-ing. • I think the artist feels …

Robert Campbell Jnr. *Aboriginal History (Facts)*, 1988

▶ SB p. 15

1 THEMES

9 LISTENING The Sapphires – a hit movie

Listen to an article about the film. Tick (✓) the correct answers.

Interaktive Übungen zu dieser Seite kannst du auf www.scook.de gratis freischalten. Deinen Code findest du auf Seite 1.

A 1 The Sapphires is

    A an American film. ☐

    B an Australian film. ✓

    C a British film. ☐

  2 The story happens in

    A the 1960s. ✓

    B the 1970s. ☐

    C the 1980s. ☐

  3 The sisters don't win the talent competition because they're

    A too young. ☐

    B not good enough. ☐

    C black. ✓

From "Sapphires" 2012

B 4 The girls want to go to Vietnam to

    A sing for US soldiers. ✓

    B fight in the war. ☐

    C go sightseeing. ☐

  5 Dave will play

    A guitar. ☐

    B keyboards. ✓

    C drums. ☐

  6 Dave says they should sing

    A country and western music. ☐

    B soul music. ✓

    C pop music. ☐

  7 Another person joins the group – it's their

    A sister. ☐

    B aunt. ☐

    C cousin. ✓

C 8 At first, the Sapphires aren't popular. True ☐ False ✓

  9 The oldest sister, Gail, gets on very well with Dave. True ☐ False ✓

 10 Suddenly, there's an attack on the camp. True ✓ False ☐

 11 The youngest sister is shot[1]. True ☐ False ✓

D 12 At the end of the film

    A Dave isn't dead – he's in hospital. He argues with Gail and leaves the group. ☐

    B Dave tells Gail he loves her and then he dies. Gail never sings again. ☐

    C Gail goes to see Dave in hospital. They've fallen in love and decide to get married. ✓

[1] shot *angeschossen*

THEMES

10 SPEAKING Asking for information
Do these role-plays with a partner.

1 An advert for members of a new band

Partner A

You're good at music and want to play in a band. You're talking to Partner B on the phone. He/She has an advert about a new band.

Ask questions to find out:
- who – looking for?
- phone number?
- when practise?
- where practise?

Partner B

You're talking to Partner A on the phone. He/She wants to play in a band. Answer his/her questions about this advert.

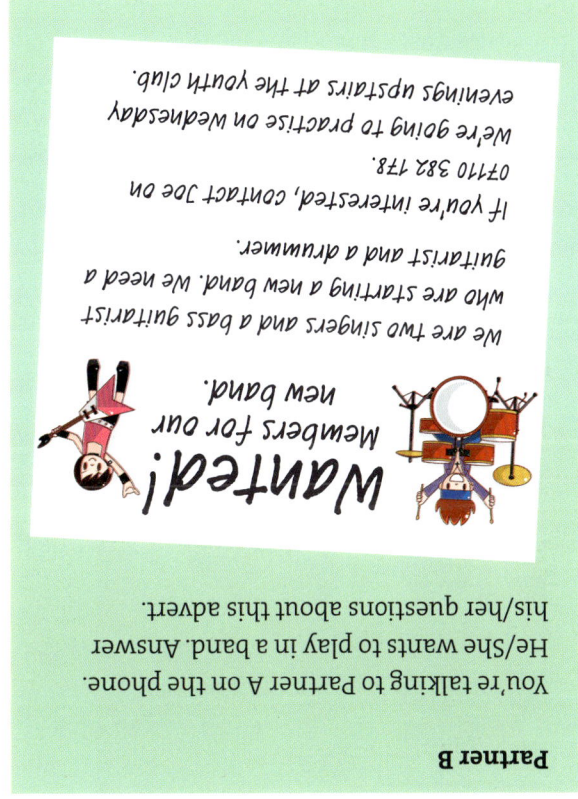

Wanted! Members for our new band.

We are two singers and a bass guitarist who are starting a new band. We need a guitarist and a drummer.
If you're interested, contact Joe on 07710 382 178.
We're going to practise on Wednesday evenings upstairs at the youth club.

2 A concert

Partner B

You're talking to Partner A on the phone. He/She wants to go out this weekend and has an advert that you might be interested in.

Ask questions to find out:
- what – advert – for?
- what kind – music?
- when?
- where?
- cost?

Partner A

You want to go out this weekend. You're talking to Partner B on the phone. Answer his/her questions about this advert.

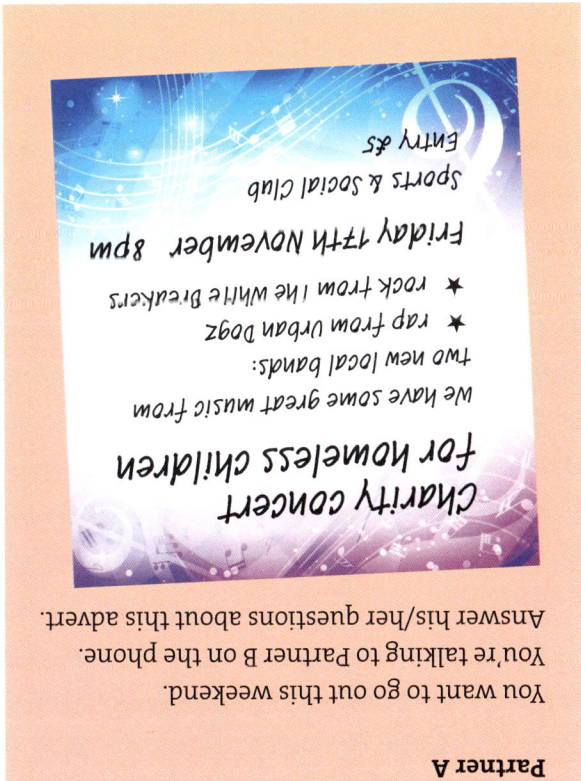

Charity concert for homeless children

We have some great music from two new local bands:
★ rap from Urban Dogz
★ rock from the White Breakers

Friday 17th November 8pm
Sports & social club
Entry £5

1 FOCUS ON LANGUAGE

11 Saving baby kangaroos [More help p.72]

Find verbs in different tenses and <u>underline</u> them in these ways:

the simple present (*what is / what happens*)

the simple past (*what happened*)   the present perfect (*what has happened*)

the going to-future (*what is going to happen*)   ● the past progressive (*what was happening*).

● (Circle) the *time words*. They help you know which **tense** to use.

> *Interaktive Übungen zu dieser Seite kannst du auf www.scook.de gratis freischalten. Deinen Code findest du auf Seite 1.*

This <u>is</u> Brolga. He <u>runs</u> a sanctuary[1] for baby kangaroos who <u>have</u> no mothers. He <u>started</u> (in 2005;) he <u>was working</u> as a tour guide when he <u>found</u> a dead kangaroo on the road. Its joey (the name for a baby kangaroo) <u>was</u> nearly dead, but Brolga <u>took</u> the joey home and <u>looked</u> after it. (Since then,) Brolga <u>has saved</u> over 200 joeys. (Now) he <u>lives</u> with about 25 kangaroos in his sanctuary in central Australia. He <u>built</u> the sanctuary himself in 2009, and now he <u>helps</u> lots of joeys (every year.) (Soon,) Brolga <u>is going to build</u> a kangaroo hospital. He <u>has</u> (already) <u>collected</u> quite a lot of money. "It's going to be a good year," <u>says</u> Brolga.

▶ SB p. 17

12 Brolga's babies [More help p.72]

Put the verbs into the right tense: simple present or simple past.

Brolga *called* (call) the first joey he *saved* (save) 'Palau' in 2005. He still *gives* (give) all his joeys names. When Palau *was* (be) one year old, Brolga *let* (let) him go free in the outback. He *wants* (want) all kangaroos to live wild if they're healthy enough. Palau *went* (go) back to the outback after one year with Brolga.

Brolga *says* (say) that he *feels* (feel) like the kangaroos' mother! He *feeds* (feed) them and they *go* (go) everywhere with him – even to the supermarket! When they're small, they *stay* (stay) inside a bag, like their mother's pouch[2].

Australian and British TV companies recently *made* (make) programmes about Brolga, and lots of people *sent* (send) money. Brolga *hopes* (hope) he can continue his work for a long time.

▶ SB p. 17

[1] sanctuary *Tierheim*   [2] pouch *Beutel*

FOCUS ON LANGUAGE

13 ◯ Mark lives in Oz
Complete the **present perfect** verbs with words from the box. You don't need two of the words.

> been • done • drunk • had • lived • played • seen • travelled • walked

I'm English, but I've _lived_ in Australia for five years now, and I've _travelled_ around quite a lot with my parents. I've _seen_ the Great Barrier Reef and I've _walked_ over the Sydney Harbour Bridge. We've _had_ barbecues on the beach at Christmas and I've _played_ cricket in the school team. But I've never _been_ to Uluru. One day I'd like to go there.

▶ SB p. 17

14 ● Megan's birthday
Put the verbs into the right tense: **present perfect** or **going to-future**.

It's my birthday tomorrow and I'_m going to go_ (go) mud racing. I've already _invited_ (invite) some friends. They'_ve_ all _done_ (do) it before. I've never _tried_ (try) it before, but I'm sure I'_m going to love_ (love) it! After the racing, we'_re going to come_ (come) back to my house. My mum _has made_ (make) a birthday cake and we'_re going to have_ (have) some pizzas too. I've already _asked_ (ask) my dad to take lots of photos.

▶ SB p. 17

15 ● Been or gone?
Read the tip. Complete the sentences with 'been' or 'gone'.

> ! be ▸ She's **been** ill three times this year.
> go ▸ She's **been** to the USA. (She went and came back.)
> go ▸ She's **gone** to Sydney. (She's still there now.)

1 Have you ever _been_ to Uluru?
2 My mum has _gone_ to Melbourne on business. She's coming back on Friday.
3 Do you know where Walid is? I can't find him and I don't know where he's _gone_.
4 I've _been_ to the new café five times already. It's really good.
5 Sam has _gone_ fishing. If you want her, you'll find her at the river.

▶ SB p. 17

16 ● What were the kangaroos doing?
Write the verbs in the **past progressive**.

When we saw the kangaroos at the sanctuary, one kangaroo _was sleeping_ (sleep) and two kangaroos _were eating_ (eat). Lots of kangaroos _were jumping_ (jump) around. One joey _was hiding_ (hide) in its mother's pouch, and two other joeys _were playing_ (play). I couldn't take any photos – I _was laughing_ (laugh) so much.

More challenge 1 p. 73 ▶ SB p. 17

eleven 11

1 FOCUS ON LANGUAGE

17 REVISION Up or down?
Complete the dialogues with the right words: up / down.

A

I'm fed *up* with this heat – I just can't cool *down*. There are no cold drinks because the fridge has broken *down*.

Oh, shut *up* and stop complaining! Let's go swimming – are you *up* for it?

B

When you've finished washing *up*, can you please tidy *up* in the living room?

Aw, Mum - I'm tired. Can't I just sit *down* and watch TV for a bit first?

18 REVISION Stars in the rainforest[1]
Read the text. Tick (✓) the correct options below.

> When you've chosen a word, read the whole sentence – is it right?

My favourite reality TV show is "I'm a Celebrity, Get Me Out of Here!". The rules are that twelve stars **1** camp in the Australian rainforest. They stay there for **2** weeks, and must do different challenges to get extra food.

I think the **3** challenge of all is when they eat insects[2] **4** are still alive[3] – yuk!!! I could **5** do that – I'd be sick! The people who do it, eat them really **6** and make funny faces! I also hate challenges with spiders and rats – I'm really scared **7** them!
I've never **8** to the rainforest, but I'd like to go one day.

1	☐ can	✓ have to	☐ should	☐ mustn't
2	☐ a bit	☐ a little	☐ a lot	✓ a few
3	☐ hardly	☐ hard	☐ harder	✓ hardest
4	☐ whose	☐ these	✓ that	☐ who
5	✓ never	☐ ever	☐ often	☐ now
6	☐ quick	✓ quickly	☐ quickness	☐ quiet
7	☐ from	✓ of	☐ for	☐ off
8	☐ be	☐ being	✓ been	☐ bye

[1] rainforest *Regenwald* [2] insect *Insekt* [3] alive *lebend*

TEXT 8, 9

19 New words puzzle
Complete the puzzle with new words from the text.

1
2  3
4 Film stars with make-up and expensive clothes look ....
5 ... car is this? It's mine!
6 Don't put your life in danger. = Don't (...) your life.
7 I want to do it! = I'm ... ...
8  9
10 (▼) 'Uluru' is the original name of the rock, given by the Indigenous Australians. The white immigrants called it _Ayers Rock_.

	1	G	O	A	T			
2	P	O	N	Y	T	A	I	L
		3	F	U	E	L		
4	G	L	A	M	O	R	O	U	S
		5	W	H	O	S	E	
			6	R	I	S	K	
		7	U	P	F	O	R	I	T
			8	C	H	I	N	
9	H	I	T	C	H	H	I	K	E	R

▶ SB p. 21

20 What do you think?   More help p. 73
Give your opinion about the story. Answer in sentences.

- What do you think of the text: the story and the characters?
- Would you like to read the book? Why / why not?
- Would you recommend[1] this book to a friend? Why / why not?
- How many stars would you give the story? ☆☆☆☆☆

▶ SB p. 21

[1] recommend _empfehlen_

1 SKILLS

My holiday down under

Last summer, I went to Australia with my mum to visit my uncle. He lives there now because his wife is Australian. I had an absolutely awesome time!

On the first day, we were very tired after our long journey, so we relaxed at my uncle's house. It's quite a big house and very modern – it was built last year. There's a large garden which even has a small swimming pool. I couldn't believe it! The weather there in August (their winter) is great. The sun shines and it's still quite hot.

The next day, we went on an exciting boat trip to the Great Barrier Reef. We had looked forward to it for months! However, my mum didn't enjoy it. For one thing, she felt sick on the boat, and she didn't like snorkelling in the sea either! But I thought it was great fun. We had hired snorkels, and flippers to wear on our feet. We looked really funny with all our gear on. The flippers were very long and I looked like a clown! But in the water, I swam like a fish, no problem. The coral and the fish on the Great Barrier Reef were totally amazing and very colourful.

In the evening, my uncle took us for a meal in his favourite restaurant. My mum had kangaroo steak, but I had a vegetarian curry. I could never eat such a beautiful animal!

At the weekend, we went to the rainforest. There were incredibly tall trees. In the morning, we went by cable car through the trees up a big hill to an Aboriginal village. I love buying souvenirs on holiday, and there were lots of tourist shops in the village, so I bought a boomerang and an Australian T-shirt.

After lunch, we visited an Aboriginal culture park. First, we watched an interesting film, then we saw a show with traditional music and dancing. After that, we had a lesson on Aboriginal hunting and we were allowed to try throwing boomerangs and spears. I had never tried it before, and it was harder than I thought!

On other days, we went to the beach, had barbecues and visited small towns nearby. It was all great, but the best thing for me was seeing the beautiful coral and the amazing fish. I had the best holiday ever – I hope I'll go back to Oz again very soon!

Jen Collins

SKILLS 1

21 READING Getting the gist
Skim through the text about Jen's holiday in Australia, then write *true* or *false*.

1 Jen really enjoyed her holiday.   *true*
2 They travelled to all the big cities.   *false*
3 Jen found some things boring.   *false*
4 They did lots of outdoor activities.   *true*

22 READING Guessing new words in the text
What do you think these words mean in German?

1 snorkelling   *schnorcheln*
2 flippers   *Schwimmflossen*
3 coral   *Koralle*
4 cable car   *Gondelbahn*

! You can often guess a new word from the context or picture, or because it's like German.

23 READING What the holiday was like
Match the sentences.

1 Jen and her mum stayed
2 The climate where Jen's uncle lives
3 Jen's mum didn't enjoy
4 Jen thought swimming with flippers
5 The fish and the coral
6 Jen bought souvenirs

A is warm and sunny.
B with Jen's uncle in Australia.
C at an Aboriginal village.
D was easy.
E the trip to the Great Barrier Reef.
F were beautiful.

1 *B*   2 *A*   3 *E*   4 *D*   5 *F*   6 *C*

24 Making a text really good

a) *Time phrases* can help a text flow well. In Jen's text, underline in blue the time phrases that tell you when things happened in the holiday.

b) Highlight *linking words* that help a text flow: and, but, so, because, however

c) Jen uses *different words* to say the same thing. Find the words she uses…

instead of 'big':
- garden – *large*
- flippers – *long*
- trees – *tall*

! Some of these are new to you. You can learn new words from texts you read!

● instead of 'very':
- holiday – *absolutely* awesome time
- swimming gear – *really* funny
- Great Barrier Reef – *totally* amazing
- rainforest trees – *incredibly* tall

d) ● Jen also uses *different verb tenses and forms*. Underline in red one example of each:
- present simple
- passive (e.g. 'was made')
- past perfect (e.g. 'had done')
- will-future

fifteen 15

1 SKILLS

 25 WRITING A holiday

a) Read the task instructions:

> **Your task:** Write about a holiday you had, or one day of a holiday.
> Include at least four of the following things:
> ★ Where were you? (country, place, accommodation)
> ★ What was it like? (weather, people, countryside)
> ★ What did you do? (activities, places)
> ★ How did you feel?
> ★ What were the best/worst things?

b) Prepare to write. These tips will help you write a good text – and do well in a writing exam!

> **A Structure your text** – Make a plan, and make notes for each part.

- Write a plan for this task in your exercise book. Make notes.
  introduction ▶ main part ▶ ending

> **B Make your text flow** – Use time phrases and linking words (see exercise 24).

- Make this flow better:
  It was sunny. We went to the beach. We had lunch. We ate in the car. It started to rain.

  > **Ideas:** after that • at 1pm • on Sunday • so • on the first day • because • but

  On Sunday it was sunny so we went to the beach. At 1pm we had lunch. We ate in the car because it started to rain.

> **C Choose your words** – Don't use the same words all the time.
> – Show what you can do: use different verb tenses.
> – If you don't know an English word, say it a different way or say something else. Don't use German!

- Improve this:
  The holiday was ~~good~~, with ~~good~~ weather. We stayed in a ~~good~~ hotel, where the food was ~~good~~.

  > **Ideas:** sunny • comfortable • perfect • fun • great • fantastic

  The holiday was fun with great weather. We stayed in a comfortable hotel where the food was fantastic.

c) Write your text in your exercise book. Use the tips and Jen's text to help you.
   Write: ○ about 100 words ● about 150 words.

> **D Check your work** – e.g. Spelling? Verb forms? Right words?
> – Have you done everything in the task?

! Sample answer p. 69

▶ SB p. 23

16 sixteen

MY LEARNER LOG

Das habe ich in Unit 1 gelernt:			
Ich kann ...	Hier habe ich's gelernt/geübt:	Und wie gut bin ich darin wirklich? Selbsteinschätzung oder Lehrereinschätzung:	Frage deine Lehrerin oder deinen Lehrer nun nach passendem Übungsmaterial:
... einem Lesetext Details entnehmen und andere darüber informieren.	S. 10–11, 16 Stop! Check! Go! 3	☺ 😐 ☹	DFF 1.1 • DFF 1.1 ⁚ DFF 1.1 ⁙
... Besuchern mein Umfeld beschreiben.	S. 11, 13 Stop! Check! Go! 5	☺ 😐 ☹	DFF 1.2 • DFF 1.2 ⁚ DFF 1.2 ⁙
... eine Radiosendung verstehen und ihr Informationen entnehmen.	S. 12, 13 Stop! Check! Go! 1	☺ 😐 ☹	DFF 1.3 • DFF 1.3 ⁚ DFF 1.3 ⁙
... Informationen von Schildern auf Deutsch und Englisch wiedergeben.	S. 13 Stop! Check! Go! 6	☺ 😐 ☹	DFF 1.4 • DFF 1.4 ⁚ DFF 1.4 ⁙
... mich in Notfallsituationen verständigen.	S. 13	☺ 😐 ☹	DFF 1.5 • DFF 1.5 ⁚ DFF 1.5 ⁙
... eine Geschichte zusammenfassen.	S. 15, 175	☺ 😐 ☹	DFF 1.6 • DFF 1.6 ⁚ DFF 1.6 ⁙
... zeitliche Bezüge verstehen und Verben in die richtigen Formen setzen.	S. 17 Stop! Check! Go! 2	☺ 😐 ☹	DFF 1.7 • DFF 1.7 ⁚ DFF 1.7 ⁙
... eine Präsentation anhand eines Networks vorbereiten und durchführen.	S. 22–23	☺ 😐 ☹	DFF 1.8 • DFF 1.8 ⁚ DFF 1.8 ⁙
... Quizfragen zu Australien beantworten.	S. 8–27, 146–147	☺ 😐 ☹	DFF 1.9 • DFF 1.9 ⁚ DFF 1.9 ⁙

Du kannst diese Seite auch in dein Dossier heften, wenn du fertig bist.

In der letzten Spalte können Sie die Schülerinnen und Schüler auf die individuell passenden Aufgaben im Material „Differenzieren Fördern Fordern" verweisen. Wird z.B. die Beherrschung der zweiten Kompetenz in Unit 1 eher mit ☺ eingeschätzt, dann passt dazu das Material 1.2 ⁙. Wahlweise können Sie in diesen Feldern auch andere geeignete Übungsaufgaben benennen.

seventeen 17

1 REVISION

1 At a café

a) Complete this dialogue in a café.

Waiter   Hello, can I <u>help</u> you?

Customer   I'd like a cheese <u>sandwich</u> and a salad, <u>please</u>.

Waiter   <u>No</u> problem. And to drink?

Customer   A coffee and a <u>bottle</u> of water, please.

Waiter   Anything <u>else</u>?

Customer   No, that's <u>all</u>, thanks.

Waiter   <u>That's</u> sixteen dollars fifty, please.

Customer   <u>Here</u> you are.

Waiter   Thanks. <u>Have</u> a nice day.

b) Write down more food and drink you can buy in a café. How many words can you write? The pictures will give you some ideas.

(soup, tea, a bottle of orange juice, fish and chips, a chicken sandwich, chocolate cake, a scone, pizza, lemonade, cola, biscuits, burgers)

c) Close your book and practise the dialogue with a partner. Change the food, drink and price each time.

d) Write a similar cafe dialogue in your exercise book. Can you do it without looking at a)?

2 Healthy or junk?

What sort of things do you eat and drink? Do you think you should change? Write sentences.

> **Useful phrases:**
> usually • sometimes • quite a lot of … • healthy / junk food • too much • not enough • more/less …

(I eat quite a lot of healthy food, but sometimes I eat junk food. For example, I often have chips and packets of crisps. I think I should probably eat more fruit and drink less cola.)

Respect

Unit 2

1 Advice about bullying
Read the advice and circle the correct words.

> To help you choose the right words, read the whole sentence.

★ If you're a person /(victim) of bullying, don't feel alone. Tell (an adult)/ a school friend you trust, for example a parent, grandparent or teacher. An adult can help you to make the problem go (away)/ out.

★ Do you have a problem with unhealthy /(horrible) phone calls? Look at the number before you (answer)/ talk the phone. If it's a number that you don't know, don't answer the (call)/ question.

★ If the problem gets really bad, you can forget /(change) your phone number (get a new SIM card) and only say /(tell) good friends your new number.

★ If you (get)/ send horrible text messages or emails, don't answer them. But don't (delete)/ read them. Keep them so that you can show them to an adult.

★ Being bullied can make you feel very happy /(unhappy). But remember, if someone is bullying you, it's not because of *you*. It's really the bully who has a problem. Perhaps the bully is clever /(jealous), or needs to feel strong, or wants to have /(hide) something negative in his or her own life.

★ Finally, don't be a (bystander)/ bully who sees bullying but says nothing. Don't just think that it's no big (deal)/ joke. Bullying can hurt people very badly. Try to find the challenge /(courage) to tell the bully that it's not fair and it's mean. Or tell an adult about it.

▶ SB p. 31

2 Positive ideas

A website about bullying says: If you're feeling unhappy, do positive things that make you feel good (and stop you thinking about bad things)!

Write five or more positive things that can make someone feel good.
Compare with your partner.

Listen to your favourite...

▶ SB p. 31

nineteen 19

2 THEMES

3 Peer pressure – a survey

a) Some words go together. Find the pairs: 1 *B* 2 *F* 3 *A* 4 *H* 5 *C* 6 *G* 7 *E* 8 *D*

1 What do you think - is peer ...
2 Can you think of one way of dealing ...
3 Most teens want to fit ...
4 Do many people in your school year smoke ...
5 Is shoplifting a big ...
6 Do you and your friends agree ...
7 Do you feel ...
8 How much are you influenced ...

A in – true or false?
B pressure a problem in school?
C issue in your area?
D by your friends?
E comfortable with most things your friends do?
F with it?
G on everything?
H cigarettes?

b) SPEAKING Ask your partner the questions from the survey in a), and say what you think too. Do you agree with your partner? [More help p.74]

What do you think? Is peer pressure a problem in school?

I disagree. I think it is a problem, especially for some younger students.

Give interesting answers – don't just say one or two words!

No, I don't think so. I don't feel any peer pressure. What about you, what do you think?

▶ SB p. 33

4 LISTENING What kinds of peer pressure?
Listen to the interview. Tick (✓) the five kinds of peer pressure Emma feels.

Listen carefully! Not everything they talk about is peer pressure.

How does Emma deal with peer pressure?

She talks to her friends about it.

▶ SB p. 33

THEMES

5 Crossword
These new words all come from pages 30–34 in your book.

Across (▶)

2 Ava goes horse-riding. Ellie wants to go, but can't. Ellie feels …

5 someone who does horrible things to another person

7 Not nice at all!

9 a person who is bullied or hurt

11 only you and me = … the two of us

13 things you're interested in, hobbies

Down (▼)

1 It's nothing important. = It's no big …

3 take something from a shop without paying

4 be there for someone, give them help

6 People who are similar to you (e.g. the same age) are your …

8 feel part of a group = … in

10 a problem or something important

12 have the same opinion about = agree …

! Games and puzzles can help you learn new words.

Across:
2 JEALOUS
5 BULLY
7 HORRIBLE
9 VICTIM
11 JUST
13 INTERESTS

Down:
1 DEAL
3 STEAL
4 SUPPORT
6 PEERS
8 FIT
10 ISSUE
12 ON

▶ SB p. 34

6 Peer pressure   More help p. 74

a) Peer pressure is when you do things because other people do them. These things are often negative, but they can be positive. How many examples can you write?

Negative peer pressure	Positive peer pressure
drugs	volunteering

 b) Compare with a partner. Can you find more examples?

▶ SB p. 34

twenty-one 21

2 THEMES

🎧 7 Racism: It stops with me.

a) The staff in an Australian office joined the anti-racism campaign. Look at the posters they made. Listen and fill in the missing words.

! Prepare yourself: Read the posters before you listen.

1 RACISM. IT STOPS WITH ME.
Our hearts are all the <u>same colour.</u>

2 RACISM. IT STOPS WITH ME.
I say no to racism! <u>Stop it now.</u>

3 RACISM. IT STOPS WITH ME.
We all smile in the <u>same language</u> ☺

4 RACISM. IT STOPS WITH ME.
<u>Say no</u> to prejudice – Respect all cultures!

5 RACISM. IT STOPS WITH ME.
– because it's what is on the inside that <u>matters</u>.

6 RACISM. IT STOPS WITH ME.
<u>Respect</u> comes first – everyone should be <u>equal</u>.

7 RACISM. IT STOPS WITH ME.
A good life is <u>for everyone.</u>

8 RACISM. IT STOPS WITH ME.
Let's not just say it – let's <u>live it.</u>

9 RACISM. IT STOPS WITH ME.
Make a better <u>society</u> where everyone feels <u>safe</u>.

b) Which three posters do you like best, and why?

_____
_____
_____

c) **MEDIATION** Explain the last four posters (6–9) in German, for a friend.

<u>6. Respekt steht an erster Stelle. Alle Menschen sollten gleich behandelt werden.</u>
<u>7. Jedem Menschen steht ein gutes Leben zu.</u>
<u>8. Nicht nur drüber reden – es leben!</u>
<u>9. Eine bessere Gesellschaft gestalten, in der sich alle sicher fühlen.</u>

▶ SB p. 35

THEMES 2

8 READING Arthur Wharton, footballing legend

It's a sad fact that even today, black footballers are called racist names during matches. However, racism isn't a new problem, and today's players are not the first to face it. But when did the world see its first black professional footballer? No, not in the 1980s. Or even the 1950s... Arthur Wharton, from West Africa, turned professional way back in 1889!

Who was Arthur Wharton? He was born in Gold Coast, now Ghana, in 1865. He came to England in 1882 to **study**, but soon found that he preferred sport. He could run very fast and won races. He was also good at cycling and cricket. But football was his main sporting career. Wharton played for many football clubs in the north of England, from 1886 until 1902. He was a great player – an excellent **goal**-keeper. Like other black people at the time, he experienced racism, but he fought back and was a proud man. Many people thought he was good enough to play for England, but he was never picked. Was this racial prejudice?

Wharton also suffered from another kind of prejudice: class. His mother had come from his country's **royalty**, but being a professional sportsman made him a **lower** class in society, so he couldn't get a job as a government **official**. At the end of his football career, Warton went to work in a **mine**. It was hard physical work. He died a poor man in 1930.

But Arthur Wharton is not forgotten! He's remembered as a footballing hero and a black hero.

a) Write the years:

1 Arthur Wharton was born in Ghana in _1865_ and he came to England in _1882_.
2 Arthur became a professional footballer in _1889_.
3 He played for clubs in the north of England from _1886 – 1902_.
4 Arthur Wharton died in _1930_.

b) Read the text. Then tick (✓) the meanings that are right for this text.

1 ✓ study *Verb* studieren   ☐ study *Substantiv* Studentenzimmer
2 ✓ goal *Substantiv* Tor   ☐ goal *Substantiv* Ziel
3 ☐ royalty *Substantiv* Tantieme   ✓ royalty *Substantiv* Mitglieder des Königshauses
4 ☐ lower *Verb* senken   ✓ lower: low *Adjektiv* niedrig
5 ✓ official *Substantiv* Beamte/Beamtin   ☐ official *Adjektiv* offiziell
6 ✓ mine *Substantiv* Bergwerk   ☐ mine *Pronomen* meiner/meine/mein(e)s

> Always look at **all** the words in a dictionary entry. Pick the best meaning.

c) ○ Circle five positive things and underline five negative things in the text.
● Write two lists in German in your exercise book: *positive* and *negative* things from the text.

▶ SB p. 36

2 FOCUS ON LANGUAGE 3, 4

9 Amy's first boyfriend

a) ⚪ Amy tells her friend about her first boyfriend, Joel. Complete what Joel said.

1. I **'m** 21 and I **work** in films.
2. I **love** driving and I **have** a sports car.
3. I **speak** five languages. I often **go** to the USA.
4. I **live** in a huge house.

! Look at pages 85–86 if you need help.

1 He said that he <u>was</u> 21 and he <u>worked</u> in films.
2 He told me that he <u>loved</u> driving and he <u>had</u> a sports car.
3 He said that he <u>spoke</u> five languages and he often <u>went</u> to the USA.
4 He told me he <u>lived</u> in a huge house.

🎧 b) In fact, it wasn't true at all! Listen and write the *true* details.
6

Joel was *15* and worked in *a DVD shop*. He didn't have a sports car – he had *a bike*. He spoke *only English* and he had never been *to another country*. He lived in *a flat* with *his mum and dad*.

▶ SB p. 39

10 ⚪ Amy's second boyfriend
Amy tells her friend about her next boyfriend, Sam. Write the correct words.

The conversation	What Amy said to her friend
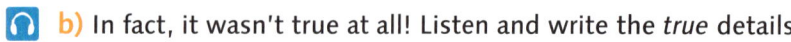	Sam was OK, but after six weeks we argued …
1 Sam I *hate your* cat.	1 He said that he *hated my* cat.
2 Amy Well *your* dog *smells* horrible!	2 So I told him that *his* dog *smelled* horrible.
3 Sam And *your* friends *are* boring.	3 And then he said that *my* friends *were* boring.
4 Amy *Your* friends *drink* too much.	4 So I said that *his* friends *drank* too much.
5 Sam I *don't like your* music.	5 He said that he *didn't like my* music.
6 Amy Yeah? *Your* music *is* rubbish!	6 I told him that *his* music *was* rubbish.
7 Sam I never *want* to see *you* again!	7 He said he never *wanted* to see *me* again!
8 Amy Well I *'m* happy with that!	8 So I said I *was* happy with that!

1 hated/hate – my/your   2 his/your – smelled/smells   3 my/your – are/were
4 your/his – drank/drink   5 don't like/didn't like – my/your   6 your/his – was/is
7 want/wanted – me/you   8 was/'m

▶ SB p. 39

24   twenty-four

FOCUS ON LANGUAGE 2

11 An internet chat

Amy tells her friend about someone she 'met' on a chat website about a sports TV show. Complete her sentences.

The boy's questions	What Amy told her friend
	At first, it was OK. He just asked questions about the show.
1 How often do you watch the sports show?	1 For example, he asked _how often I watched the sports show._
2 Do you do any sports?	2 He asked _if I did any sports._
3 Do you go dancing?	3 Then he asked other things. He asked _if I went dancing._
4 What music do you like?	4 And he asked _what music I liked._
5 What's your mobile number?	5 Then he asked _what my mobile number was._
6 Where do you live?	6 And he wanted to know _where I lived._ I didn't tell him.
7 When does school finish?	7 He wanted to know _when school finished._
8 Do you have any photos of you in a bikini?	8 I didn't answer his questions. But then he asked _if I had any photos of me in a bikini._ It was horrible! I thought – who is this guy? So I told my mum.

▶ SB p. 40

12 Advice from Amy's mum

Amy tells her friend what her mum said. Complete her sentences.

I'm really glad I talked to my mum about it. She told me _not to worry._ She also told me _to stop using the website._ Of course, she told me _not to give anyone my address or phone number._ I'm glad I didn't. She told me _to report the guy to the website owners._ And she told me _to be careful online_ and _not to meet with anyone._ She's right. You don't know who these people really are...

More challenge 2 p. 75 ▶ SB p. 40

twenty-five 25

2 FOCUS ON LANGUAGE

13 REVISION Word families

a) Look at the families of words below and put them in the right places in the table below.

- train training trained trainer
- tidied tidy tidy
- teach taught teacher
- help helpful help helper helped
- work worked worker work
- sleep sleepy slept sleep
- owned own owner
- song sang singer sing

person (noun)	thing (noun)	what people do (verb: simple pres.)	what someone did (verb: simple past)	describing (adjective)
trainer	training	train	trained	—
—	—	tidy	tidied	tidy
teacher	—	teach	taught	—
helper	help	help	helped	helpful
worker	work	work	worked	—
—	sleep	sleep	slept	sleepy
owner	—	own	owned	—
singer	song	sing	sang	—

b) ● Write these words in the table below. [More help p.76]

- write   friendship   meeting   visit   clean   dance

How many other words do you know in the same family? Write them in the table too.

person (noun)	thing (noun)	what people do (verb: simple pres.)	what someone did (verb: simple past)	describing (adjective)
writer	—	write	wrote	—
friend	friendship	—	—	friendly
—	meeting	meet	met	—
visitor	visit	visit	visited	—
—	—	clean	cleaned	clean
dancer	dance	dance	danced	—

👥 Does your partner have any words that you don't have?

TEXT

14 Watching you, watching me: What happens next?

What do you think will happen next in the story? Write sentences.

Ideas:
Natasha's dad   say 'sorry' to…   meet…
Natasha   Matt   will   come and live in… talk to…
Matt's parents   fall in love with… argue with…

Matt's parents will come and live in the house.
Matt will meet Natasha.
Natasha's dad will say 'sorry' to Matt.
Natasha will fall in love with Matt.

▶ SB p. 43/p. 116

15 What do these new words mean?

More help   p.76

Complete the sentences.

1 A **squatter** is someone who lives in *an empty house*.
2 A **tramp** is someone who *doesn't have a home*.
3 To **hammer** on a door means to knock *very loudly*.
4 You can use a **candle** if the lights in the house *don't work*.
5 When you close the **curtains**, people can't *look into the house*.
6 "I **have every right to** be here" means *"I'm allowed to be here"*.
7 A **busybody** is *someone who is nosey*.

▶ SB p. 43/p. 116

16 Squatters: your opinion

Matt isn't a squatter. But what do you think about squatters? Write your opinion.

Some useful words and phrases:
in my opinion • I think • (don't) have the right to • should/shouldn't • live in empty houses • rent/buy • like other people • fair/unfair • enough money/houses • be homeless • make a mess • empty house • a waste • belongs to • not theirs

▶ SB p. 43/p. 116

2 SKILLS

Please, Mum, Dad – can I …?

"When I ask my parents for something, they usually say 'no' and we always end up arguing." Is this true for you? What can you do to have a better chance of success?

Prepare well

1. **Make sure what you ask for is reasonable[1].** Are you asking to stay out until midnight on a school night? Of course your parents will say no! If you're asking for too much pocket money, maybe you should get a part-time job or offer to do some chores round the house to earn the money?

2. **Choose the most important thing**, and ask for that. Don't suddenly ask your parents for lots of things, large and small.

3. **Show your parents that they can trust you**, before you ask. For example, you're allowed to come home at 9 pm on weekdays, but you want to change that to 9.30 pm. Well, don't keep coming in at 9.15 pm – that will just irritate your parents and they won't trust you.

4. **Choose the best time.** Don't ask your parents for something when they're busy or stressed. They're more likely to say 'no' and not listen properly to what you say. Choose a time when they're calm and relaxed. Make sure you're calm too, so you won't start to argue with your parents.

Talking with your parents

5. **Say what you'd like and explain why.** If you're asking your parents for more pocket money, show them a list of what you spend your money on, and the things you need extra money for.
Don't just say: "All my friends do this! All my friends have that!". You can guess what your parents will answer: "If your friends jumped off a bridge, would you do that too?"!

6. **Listen to what your parents say.** After all, you want them to listen to you. And show them you've listened to their point of view: "I know you worry about my safety when I come home late, but there's a bus at 10.40, and Richie and Jen are going to the party and they'll get the same bus."

7. **You might have to compromise[2].** For example, you can usually stay out until 10.30 pm at the weekend, and you're asking for 1am this Saturday. Your parents say midnight… Well, that's not bad. It's still a lot later than usual.

8. **Don't argue – discuss!** Stay calm and don't shout. Don't be rude or aggressive. Your parents will just say no. If you roll your eyes or argue "That's so unfair! You never listen to me! You don't care!", you've lost. Your parents will think you're still a child.

9. **Always do what you say you'll do.** If you say you'll wash up every day for more pocket money, don't forget and don't just do it at the weekend. Keep your promises and your parents will keep theirs.

---

[1] reasonable *vernünftig* [2] compromise *Kompromisse schließen*

SKILLS

17 READING Getting the gist
Skim through the article on page 28. Which summary is best: A, B or C? _A_

A The article gives advice to teenagers: how to ask their parents for things successfully.

B The article tells parents how to talk to their teenage children without arguing.

C The article shows the difficult problems that many families have.

18 READING Dos and Don'ts
What advice does the article give? Write 'True' or 'False'.

Part 1 You shouldn't ask for too much pocket money. Your parents will probably say no. _True_

Part 2 It's best to ask for everything you want at one time, so you only have to ask once. _False_

Part 4 Ask for something when your parents are busy. They won't think and will just say yes. _False_

Part 5 It's a good idea to tell your parents what all your friends are allowed to do. _False_

Part 8 Don't just accept what your parents say. If you argue and shout, they'll listen to you. _False_

Part 9 If you promise to do something, it's important to do it. _True_

19 LISTENING Do they follow the advice?
Listen to parts of conversations between teens and their parents. For each piece of advice read the paragraph in the article again. Do the teens follow the advice? Tick (✓) ☺ or ☹.

> ! You're listening for the gist here – not for individual words that tell you the answer.

Advice from the article:	☺	☹
1 Make sure what you ask for is reasonable.		✓
2 Choose the most important thing.		✓
3 Show your parents that they can trust you.	✓	
4 Choose the best time.		✓
5 Say what you'd like and explain why.	✓	
6 Listen to what your parents say.	✓	
7 You might have to compromise.	✓	
8 Don't argue – discuss!		✓
9 Always do what you say you'll do.		✓

20 What do you think?
Write your opinions in your exercise book.

- Does the article give good advice? What advice will you try to remember?
- What time should teens of your age be allowed to come home on week nights? And at the weekend?
- How much time should teens be allowed to spend each day on a computer? And on a mobile phone?

twenty-nine

2 SKILLS

21 READING Asking for something

a) Do these role-plays with a partner.

1 A discussion that goes badly ☹

Partner A – teenager

You want to come home at 11.30 pm on Saturday.
You ask your mum/dad (Partner B).

- Start the conversation and ask your question.
- Say why (party).
- pick up in car?
- not fair! not a child!
- End the conversation.

Partner B – parent

Partner A is your teenage son/daughter and asks to stay out late.

- why?
- too late
- no way!
- for the last time – no!

2 A discussion that goes well ☺

Partner A – parent

Partner B is your teenage son/daughter and wants more pocket money.

- why need more?
- will have to help more in the house
- when start?
- OK

Partner B – teenager

You want more pocket money.
You ask your mum / dad (Partner A).

- Start the conversation and ask your question.
- Say why you need extra money.
- Say what you can do.
- Answer their questions.
- End the conversation.

 b) **WRITING** Write two dialogues in your exercise book.

1: The teenager wants to stay out very late. The conversation goes well.
2: The teenager wants more pocket money. The conversation goes badly.

c) Read your dialogues with a partner. Act the roles.

! Sample answer: p. 69

! For ideas look at the article on p. 28 and listen to exercise 19 again.

30 thirty

MY LEARNER LOG

Das habe ich in Unit 2 gelernt:			
Ich kann …	Hier habe ich's gelernt/geübt:	Und wie gut bin ich darin wirklich? Selbsteinschätzung oder Lehrereinschätzung:	Frage deine Lehrerin oder deinen Lehrer nun nach passendem Übungsmaterial:
… einem Hörtext über *bullying* Informationen entnehmen.	S. 30–31, 34 Stop! Check! Go! 3	😊 😐 ☹	DFF 2.1 • DFF 2.1 ⚁ DFF 2.1 ⚄
… einen Kommentar verfassen.	S. 33, 110 Stop! Check! Go! 5	😊 😐 ☹	DFF 2.2 • DFF 2.2 ⚁ DFF 2.2 ⚄
… ein Problem im Gespräch lösen.	S. 34	😊 😐 ☹	DFF 2.3 • DFF 2.3 ⚁ DFF 2.3 ⚄
… Begriffe zum Wortfeld *discrimination* anwenden.	S. 30–37	😊 😐 ☹	DFF 2.4 • DFF 2.4 ⚁ DFF 2.4 ⚄
… Gesagtes in indirekter Rede wiedergeben *(reported speech)*.	S. 38–40 Stop! Check! Go! 1	😊 😐 ☹	DFF 2.5 • DFF 2.5 ⚁ DFF 2.5 ⚄
… Gesagtes in indirekter Rede wiedergeben *(backshift of tenses in reported speech)*.	S. 40, 114 Stop! Check! Go! 1	😊 😐 ☹	DFF 2.6 • DFF 2.6 ⚁ DFF 2.6 ⚄
… einem Lesetext über *bullying* Informationen entnehmen.	S. 32–33, 35, 41–43 Stop! Check! Go! 2	😊 😐 ☹	DFF 2.7 • DFF 2.7 ⚁ DFF 2.7 ⚄
… höfliche Gespräche auf Englisch führen.	S. 44–45 Stop! Check! Go! 6 & 7	😊 😐 ☹	DFF 2.8 • DFF 2.8 ⚁ DFF 2.8 ⚄
… einem Lesetext Informationen entnehmen und durch *participles* knapper formulieren.	S. 50–51	😊 😐 ☹	DFF 2.9 • DFF 2.9 ⚁ DFF 2.9 ⚄

Du kannst diese Seite auch in dein Dossier heften, wenn du fertig bist.

2 REVISION

1 TV shows

a) Write these TV programmes and find the right picture.

1 scnc fctn flm – _science fiction film – E_
2 crtn – _cartoon – H_
3 tlk shw – _talk show – A_
4 hrrr flm – _horror film – C_
5 cmdy – _comedy – F_
6 msc prgrmm – _music programme – D_
7 rlty shw – _reality show – G_
8 sprts shw – _sports show – B_

b) Write three more sorts of TV programme that you know.

2 Opinions about TV

Write about eight sorts of TV programme in your exercise book. The table will help you.

I mostly/often/sometimes/never	watch		because	relaxing/stupid/…
I love/enjoy/quite like/hate	watching	…	they're	
			I find them	

3 A reality show

a) Adjectives and adverbs. (Circle) the right words.

I saw a very (**good**)/ well reality show. Twelve people were put on an island. They had to find food and water quick /(**quickly**), and it wasn't (**easy**)/ easily. They had to be (**careful**)/ carefully, because it's (**dangerous**)/ dangerously to drink dirty water. At first, the people argued angry /(**angrily**) with each other. They made a fire, but there was a (**terrible**)/ terribly tropical storm and it rained heavy /(**heavily**) – and their fire went out. Lucky /(**Luckily**), things got better on the second day.

b) Complete the sentences with a good adjective or adverb.

They were very _(happy)_ because they found water. They put some in bottles and carried them back _(carefully)_, trying not to drop any. But it wasn't _(clean)_ water so they had to boil it on the fire. On the fourth day, they saw a _(small)_ rabbit in the _(dark)_ forest. They crept up _(quietly)_, but one of the people saw a _(big)_ snake and shouted _(loudly)_ and the rabbit ran away. They had nothing to eat and were very _(hungry)_.

Looking forward

Unit 3

1 Chores in the house
Write a phrase for each picture. Use these verbs:

set   wash   clean   iron   use   empty   tidy   use

1 <u>use the washing machine</u>
2 <u>iron (my) clothes</u>
3 <u>set the table</u>
4 <u>use the vacuum cleaner</u>
5 <u>empty the dishwasher</u>
6 <u>tidy up / tidy my room</u>
7 <u>wash the car</u>
8 <u>clean the bathroom</u>

▶ SB p. 53

2 Food and money
a) Read the meanings and write the words. They are all on page 52 in your book.

Food   It's a hot meal that you can buy to eat at home: <u>a takeaway</u>

It's something you eat with pasta. It often has tomatoes in it: <u>sauce</u>

It's the text that tells you how to cook a meal: <u>recipe</u>

They are the different foods that you need to make a meal: <u>ingredients</u>

Money   It's when you spend more money than you wanted to: <u>overspend</u>

It's when you spend all your money, so you have none: <u>run out of money</u>

It's when you plan how much money to spend on different things: <u>budget</u>

It's when you get money for work you've done: <u>earn money</u>

b) Write the meaning of these new words (from pages 52 and 53):

1 college   <u>a place where some people go after school</u>
2 do the shopping   <u>buy things you need</u>
3 life skills   <u>things you have to be able to do</u>

▶ SB p. 53

3 Learn the words!
Do you know the words in exercises 1 & 2?
Practise the words you don't remember.
Learn them in a sentence, e.g. *I never clean the bathroom; I can make a great cheese sauce.*

! Ask a partner to test you.

thirty-three 33

3 THEMES

4 Describing people
Read what these students say. Which adjective describes each person?

careful • confident • energetic • enthusiastic • helpful • polite • punctual • reliable

1. I'm never late for school. I always arrive 10 minutes early.
punctual

2. Of course I'll come to every football practice. If I say I'll be there, I *will* be there.
reliable

3. I can speak French pretty well. When I go to Paris, I'll be OK.
confident

4. Could I borrow your book, please? Would you mind? ... Oh, thank you very much.
polite

5. I've just played basketball, and now I'm going to go jogging. Then I'll walk into town.
energetic

6. I'm learning to play the flute. It's awesome – I really love it! I practise for hours every day.
enthusiastic

7. Are you finding the homework difficult? Here, let me show you how to do it...
helpful

8. I always think about what I'm writing, and I check my work. I don't want to make mistakes.
careful

▶ SB p. 55

5 What job is it?   More help p. 77

a) Choose four jobs from the list below. Write the qualities you think are needed for each job – but don't write the name of the job! Write in your exercise book.

Example: *To be a _____ you need to be helpful and patient, and have good communication skills. You have to like young people. And you should be good at maths!*

! You can find useful words on pp. 56 and 57 in your book and in Wordbank 2 on p. 143.

painter	doctor	mechanic
pilot	receptionist	florist
singer	soldier	bank manager
web designer	cook	baker

b) Your partner reads your descriptions and writes the names of the jobs.

Example: *To be a maths teacher you need to be...*

▶ SB p. 55

THEMES

6 What's my job?

The game: you're going to ask 'yes'/'no' questions to guess someone's job.

a) PREPARE Work with a partner.
How many ways can you find to finish these questions? Write in your exercise book.

Example: *Do you work ... inside / in an office / with animals /*

1 Do you work...?
2 Do you wear...?
3 Do you need to be...?
4 Do you need to have...?

> **Some Ideas:**
> good communication skills • in a team • shifts • with people • special clothes • special training • at weekends • calm • outside • a uniform • a qualification polite • special equipment • ... • ...

b) PRACTISE Listen to British students playing the game.

8
- What is each person's job? Did you guess before the British students?

1 *farmer* 3 *doctor*
2 *football coach* 4 *police officer*

- Listen again. Do you hear any questions that aren't on your list? Write them down.

c) PLAY the game in pairs or small groups.
Choose a job from the Wordbank on page 144 in your book.
Your partner asks 'yes/no' questions. Can he or she guess the job?
How many questions does he or she need?
Play again. Now your partner can choose.

▶ SB p. 57

3 THEMES

7 An interesting job
Listen to the radio interview. Make notes in the grid.

! Read the instructions carefully. You only have to write notes, not sentences.

1 How long Max has been a movie extra:	three and a half years
2 What a movie extra is:	background actor in a TV show
3 Does a movie extra speak?	no
4 Qualities you need to be a movie extra: ○ 3 qualities ● 5 qualities	hard-working, energetic, reliable, punctual, enthusiastic
5 Where you might work:	in the TV studios, sometimes outside, in the street or in the country
6 Why you need your own transport:	The day starts very early, when there are no buses.
7 Disadvantages of the job: ○ 1 disadvantage ● 2 disadvantages	You don't earn very much. Sometimes there's no work for weeks.
8 Why Max likes being a movie extra: ○ 1 reason ● 2 reasons	great fun; every job is different

8 MEDIATION Advice for movie extras
Explain this advice to a friend in German.

! Use a dictionary for important words if you need to.

! **Top tips for movie extras**
- Turn off your phone and don't chat while you're working!
- Listen carefully to instructions.
- Don't look at the camera!
- Don't stop acting till they shout: "Cut".

THEMES

9 A job for you?
Would you like to be a movie extra? Why/why not? Write in your exercise book:
- ○ 1 sentence   ● 3 sentences or more.

10 An application form
Fill in this application form for a part-time job in a shop.

> You can write it for yourself, or you can make up the details (e.g. for a famous person)!

> - Use a dictionary if you don't understand all the words.
> - Don't use short forms.
> - Always check your spelling.

Job Application Form

Family name: _____   First name(s): _____

Date of birth: _____   Sex: Male / Female

Address: _____

_____   Mobile no.: _____

Nationality: _____

First language: _____

Other languages: _____

Qualities and key skills: _____

_____

_____

Work experience: _____

_____

_____

Interests and achievements: _____

_____

_____

▶ SB p. 58

3 FOCUS ON LANGUAGE

11 A new friend
First read the answers. Then complete the questions with a question word.

1 _What_ hobbies do you have? – I play tennis and badminton.
2 _Where_ do you play? – At a sports club in the nearest town.
3 _How_ do you get there? – My dad takes me in the car.
4 _When_ do you play? – I play every weekend.
5 _Why_ do you prefer badminton? – Because it's a faster game.

▶ SB p.61

12 Questions for your partner
More help p.77
Write these questions.

1 Saturday? • do • What • you • last • did
What did you do last Saturday?

2 at • you • sport? • good • Are
Are you good at sport?

3 you • match? • a • been • football • Have • to
Have you been to a football match?

4 watch • evening? • you • Did • yesterday • TV
Did you watch TV yesterday evening?

5 your • Who • singer? • favourite • is
Who is your favourite singer?

6 do • you • How many • have? • video games
How many video games do you have?

! Ask your partner the questions. How many of your answers are the same?

▶ SB p.61

13 A phone call
Complete the questions with: is / are / was / were. Use the same tense as in the answer.

1 Where _are_ you at the moment? – I'm at the sports club.
2 _Is_ Jen at the sports club too? – Yes, she is.
3 Where _were_ you last night? – I was at a party.
4 _Was_ Zack at the party? – Yes, he was.
5 _Were_ Jo and Matt there too? – No, they weren't.
6 Where _are_ they today? – Why do you want to know where everybody is? Don't be so nosey!

! **Questions with the verb 'to be'**
Usual forms of the verb – different word order!
I am ▸ Am I late?
She was ▸ Where was she?

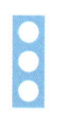

▶ SB p.61

FOCUS ON LANGUAGE

14 Questions for a young athlete

a) Complete the sentences with: do / does / did.

1 *Do* you run every day? – Yes, I run every day.

2 *Did* you run when you were at school?
 – Yes, I started when I was 12.

3 When *did* you win your first race?
 – When I was 14.

4 *Do* your brothers and sisters do any sport?
 – My brother plays football.

5 *Does* he play in a team? – Yes, he's very good.

b) Look at the answers and write the questions.

1 How many races *have you won*? – Oh, I've won lots of races!

2 When *did you join* your club? – I joined when I was 15.

3 *Does your trainer help* you a lot?
 – Yes, my trainer helps me very much.

4 *Will you race* in the next Olympics?
 – I'll race if they pick me for the team!

5 *Do you eat* healthy food?
 – Yes, I eat very healthy food.

6 *Are you going to have a rest* after this competition?
 – I'm going to have a couple of days off. Then it's back to my training!

> **Questions with other verbs**
> Usual forms of the verb – different word order!
> you are going ▸ Where are you going?
> you will do ▸ What will you do?
> you have been ▸ Have you been away?
> Except in the **simple present** and **simple past**.
> Here you use do / does / did
> you play ▸ Do you play?
> he plays ▸ Does he play?
> you played ▸ Did you play?

▸ SB p. 61

15 Questions for a famous person. More help p. 78

a) Choose a famous person.
In your exercise book, write ten questions you'd like to ask him/her.

> **Ideas:**
> How old? • Married? • Husband/wife? •
> How many children? • Names? •
> Where live? • Job?

b) Then find the answers on the internet, and complete the interview.

The Duke of Cambridge works as a co-pilot for the East Anglian Air Ambulance.

More challenge 3 p. 79 ▸ SB p. 61

3 FOCUS ON LANGUAGE

16 ⊙ **REVISION** How big? How often? How much? How many?
Put these words in order in their groups.

1	2	3	4
large small huge quite big	sometimes often never always	not very quite extremely very	a few people nobody everybody many people

1 _small_ — quite big — _large_ — _huge_

2 never — _sometimes_ — _often_ — _always_

3 not very — _quite_ — _very_ — extremely

4 _nobody_ — a few people — _many people_ — everybody

17 REVISION Words that go together in phrases

a) Write the words that go with each verb.

> ~~home~~ • lunch • ~~crazy~~ • to sleep • a message • by bus • an idea • it easy • away • fun • notes • a photo • shopping • a party • a sore leg • for it! • wrong • risks • for a walk • your temperature • every right to • out • a good day • part in • to bed • swimming

1 GO … _home / crazy / to sleep / by bus / away / shopping / for it! / wrong / for a walk / out / to bed / swimming_

2 TAKE … _a message / it easy / notes / a photo / risks / your temperature / part in_

3 HAVE … _lunch / an idea / fun / a party / a sore leg / every right to / a good day_

b) ⊙ Challenge: Write two sentences with phrases from a). How many can you put in?

Example: I've decided to go for it and take part in a 15 km race for charity. I'm sure I'll have a good day
— I just hope I don't have sore legs after the race!

40 forty

TEXT

18 Word puzzles

a) Find these words in the story. The last letter of each word is the first letter of the next.

- Not a lie – the ...
- I'm sixteen and six months. = I'm sixteen and a ...
- To apply for a job, you have to fill in an application ...
- Cindy put ... on her face to make her look older.
- She also decided to ... her hair back.
- She wore ... on her lips.
- Cal wanted to ... Cindy, but she pulled back.

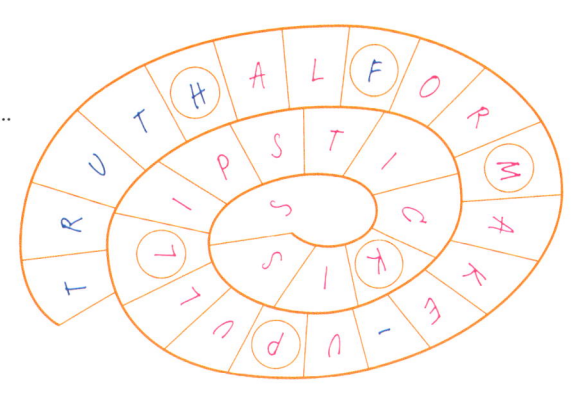

b) These words from the text all begin with 'C'.

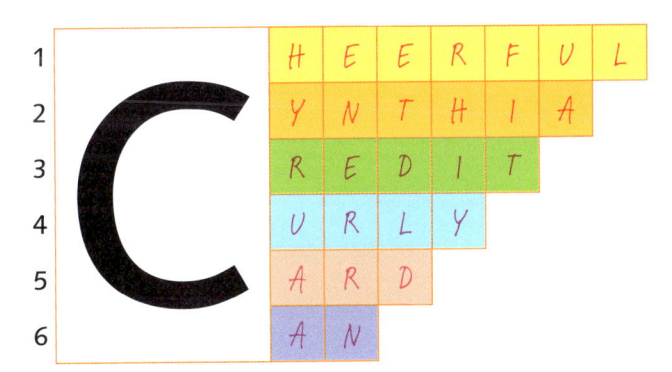

#	Letters	Clue
1	HEERFUL	This is another word for happy.
2	YNTHIA	This is the name Cindy used at the hotel.
3	REDIT	3 & 5 You can pay with a ... ...
4	URLY	The hotel manager had ... brown hair.
5	ARD	
6	AN	I'd like a ... of cola, please.

▶ SB p. 65/p. 132

19 What's the message?

What do you think is the message of the story?

☐ 1 If you tell lies, you won't get the best boyfriend/girlfriend.

☐ 2 If you tell a small lie, nobody will mind, and you can get a great job.

☑ 3 If you start with one lie, you'll have to tell lots more lies that you don't want to tell.

▶ SB p. 65/p. 132

20 Truth or lie?

What would you do or say in these situations, and why? Write in your exercise book.

I'd probably ... / I think I'd ... / I'd definitely ... / I wouldn't ... because

1 ... if you really needed some money, but were a year too young for the part-time job you wanted?

2 ... if you lost the expensive new jacket that your dad had given you for Christmas?

3 ... if your friend asked if you liked his/her new clothes – and you really didn't?

4 ... if your best friend asked you to help with a problem, but you really wanted to watch TV?

! Sample answer: p. 70

▶ SB p. 65/p. 132

3 SKILLS

Readers' real life experiences!

This week: My first day at work

We asked you to write in and tell us of your experiences on your first day at work. Here are some of the stories you sent us.

I didn't meet the manager at my job interview because she was away on business. I was introduced to all the staff, and they were very friendly. On my first morning, a young woman arrived at the same time as me. I said, "Is it your first day too? Don't be nervous, they're very nice here." The woman said "No, it isn't my first day. I'm the manager!" I just wanted to die!

Emily R

When I arrived at work on my first day, the company had just won a prize for something, so everyone was happy. We all drank champagne, and the boss[1] took us out for lunch. What a great way to start!

Nabila H

Forty years ago, on my first morning at work, a pretty girl smiled at me in the lift. We started to chat. One year later, we got married! Now we have six beautiful grandchildren.

Frank McL

On my first day as a trainee painter and decorator, my boss[1] told me to go to the shop and buy blue paint[2] with red stripes in it. I was so young and nervous, I just did what I was told. But when everyone in the shop laughed at me, I suddenly saw the joke – of course there's no such thing as striped paint! I felt so stupid.

Janek K

I had a Saturday job in a hotel. On my first day, we were very busy, and I had to make about ten ham[3] salads for lunch. I took one of the two big pieces of ham out of the fridge, and cut it into slices on the machine. The next day, the manager asked me, "Do you like raw[4] ham, Sarah?" I said I'd never tried it. "Well, that's what you gave our guests," he said. "You took the wrong ham from the fridge. That piece wasn't cooked!" For the rest of the week, I was worried that our guests would be ill! But luckily nobody complained.

Sarah B

On my first morning at work, I wanted to make a good impression[5]. I wore new trousers and a jacket, and I pretended I was grown-up[6] and confident. But when I sat down at my desk, the chair broke and I fell onto the floor, with my legs in the air! I wasn't hurt, but I had to walk around for the rest of the day with a huge hole in the back of my trousers! Well, it gave me something to laugh about with my new colleagues[7] …

Lucas W

---

[1] boss *Chef/Chefin*   [2] paint *Farbe*   [3] ham *Schinken*   [4] raw *roh*   [5] impression *Eindruck*   [6] grown-up *erwachsen*
[7] colleague *Kollege/Kollegin*

SKILLS

21 ⭕ **READING** Embarrassing or good?
Skim through the stories quickly. Does each person tell about an embarrassing thing or a good thing on their first day at work?

> ❗ You don't need to understand every word.

	embarrassing	good		embarrassing	good
Emily R	✓		Frank McL	✓	
Nabila H		✓	Sarah B		✓
Janek K	✓		Lucas W	✓	

22 ⭕ **READING** Which person is it?
Write the name of the person.

1 Which person's boss played a trick on him? *Janek K*
2 Who had a small accident? *Lucas W*
3 Who met his future wife? *Frank McL*
4 Which person's office was celebrating something? *Nabila H*
5 Who said something embarrassing to the boss? *Emily R*
6 Who made a mistake in the kitchen? *Sarah B*

> ❗ If you're not sure of some answers, do the ones you can do first, then go back to the harder ones.

23 **Your favourite story**
Which story is your favourite? Why?

___

24 **MEDIATION** Explain a story
Choose a story: ⭕ Frank's or Nabila's / 🔵 Janek's or Lucas'.
Explain the story in German, for a friend.

> ❗ You don't have to translate every word.

forty-three 43

3 SKILLS

25 WRITING Writing about a job

a) Choose task 1 <u>or</u> 2.

Task 1: My first day
Write a letter to a magazine about your first day at a job.
It can be real, or you can make up¹ the details.
Write about:
- ★ what the job was,
- ★ what the other people were like,
- ★ what you had to do,
- ★ how your first day went (well? / badly?),
- ★ and what happened.

Task 2: An interesting job
Write an article for the school magazine about an interesting job.
Write about:
- ★ what the job is,
- ★ what you have to do in this job,
- ★ the working hours and what you earn,
- ★ positive and negative things about the job,
- ★ and if you'd like this job.

b) Prepare to write. You can use a dictionary to find the name of the job.
Remember the tips from unit 1:

A **Stucture your text** — Make a plan, and make notes for each part.

B **Make your text flow** — Use time phrases *(first, then, ...)* and linking words *(because, but, ...)*

C **Choose your words** — Don't use the same words all the time – use different words
  (e.g. good, nice, great, fun, interesting, enjoyable).
  – Show what you can do: use different verb tenses and forms
  *(e.g. I'd never tried that before, I was introduced to the others,
  next time I'll..., if I had the chance, I'd like to...).*

c) Write your letter or article in your exercise book.
Write: ◯ about 100 words ● about 150 words.

D **Check your work** — Is the spelling correct?
  – Are the verb forms correct?
  – Have you used the right words?
  – Have you done everything in the task?

! Sample answers: p.70

¹ make up *erfinden*

MY LEARNER LOG

Das habe ich in Unit 3 gelernt:			
Ich kann ...	Hier habe ich's gelernt/geübt:	Und wie gut bin ich darin wirklich? Selbsteinschätzung oder Lehrereinschätzung:	Frage deine Lehrerin oder deinen Lehrer nun nach passendem Übungsmaterial:
... eine Person beschreiben.	S. 54 Stop! Check! Go! 5	☺ 😐 ☹	DFF 3.1 DFF 3.1 DFF 3.1
... Begriffe aus dem Wortfeld *jobs* anwenden.	S. 56–57	☺ 😐 ☹	DFF 3.2 DFF 3.2 DFF 3.2
... Stellenanzeigen Informationen entnehmen und passenden Personenbeschreibungen zuordnen.	S. 54–57 Stop! Check! Go! 4	☺ 😐 ☹	DFF 3.3 DFF 3.3 DFF 3.3
... eine Präsentation über einen Traumjob halten.	S. 56–57	☺ 😐 ☹	DFF 3.4 DFF 3.4 DFF 3.4
... mich um einen Job bewerben.	S. 58–59 Stop! Check! Go! 2 & 3	☺ 😐 ☹	DFF 3.5 DFF 3.5 DFF 3.5
... die wesentlichen Inhalte einer Stellenanzeige auf Deutsch oder Englisch vermitteln.	S. 59	☺ 😐 ☹	DFF 3.6 DFF 3.6 DFF 3.6
... Fragen formulieren und beantworten.	S. 52–53, 60–61 Stop! Check! Go! 1	☺ 😐 ☹	DFF 3.7 DFF 3.7 DFF 3.7
... einem Vorstellungsgespräch wesentliche Informationen entnehmen.	S. 55, 66 Stop! Check! Go! 6a & b	☺ 😐 ☹	DFF 3.8 DFF 3.8 DFF 3.8
... ein Vorstellungsgespräch führen.	S. 66–67 Stop! Check! Go! 6c & 7	☺ 😐 ☹	DFF 3.9 DFF 3.9 DFF 3.9
... *question tags* korrekt anwenden.	S. 73	☺ 😐 ☹	DFF 3.10 DFF 3.10 DFF 3.10

Du kannst diese Seite auch in dein Dossier heften, wenn du fertig bist.

3 REVISION

1 Your school
a) Match the questions and answers. Draw lines.

1 How big is your school? — c) There are over ... students.
2 How old are the students? — a) They're from ... to ... years old.
3 How long is the school day? — f) It starts at ... and ends at ...
4 How much homework do you get? — d) We get about ... hours each night.
5 Are there clubs after school? — g) There are lots, for example the ... club and the ...
6 Is there a school uniform? — e) No there isn't, but students aren't allowed to wear ...
7 Are mobile phones allowed? — b) No, not in lessons, but they're allowed...

b) Write the questions and answers about your school in your exercise book.

2 School subjects: good, better, best
a) (Circle) the right form of the adjectives.

For me, the **(easiest)** / easy / easier subject is art, because I'm quite best / **(good)** / better at drawing. I think the harder / hard / **(hardest)** subject is P.E. I'm very **(bad)** / worst / worse at all sports. I like languages, and I find that German is easy / easiest / **(easier)** than French. Geography is OK, but it's difficult / **(more difficult)** / most **difficult** than history. My **(best)** / good / better teacher is Mrs Simpson – she's great.

b) Write a similar paragraph about yourself and school subjects.

3 English lessons
a) What do you do in English lessons? Find verbs that fit the sentences.

1 We *learn* words and phrases by heart[1].
2 We *read* stories and articles.
3 We sometimes *work* with a partner.
4 We *listen* to English conversations on CD.
5 We *write* sentences and texts.
6 We try to *say* words with a good accent.

b) Write your opinion of five things you do in English lessons in your exercise book.

Example: I enjoy work**ing** with a partner and in groups.
Read**ing** stories is fun.

! Remember to use the ...ing form!

> I enjoy / I prefer / I like / I'm good at / I'm not so good at / I'm better at + ... ing.
> ...ing is interesting / fun / very difficult / quite easy.
> ...ing is more fun / harder / than + ...ing.

[1] by heart *auswendig*

Generation *like*

Unit 4

1 What is it to be cool?

a) Listen to these teenagers and fill in the missing words.

> At the end, read the sentences and check. Are your words right for the context?

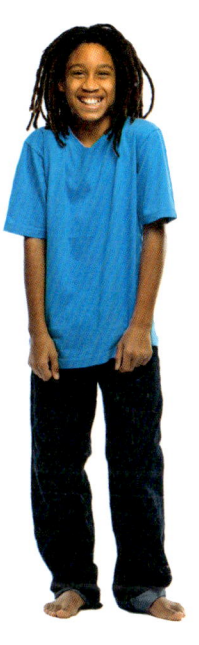

1 Lucy
Some people think that *following fashion* is cool. But I totally disagree. I think it's much better to have your own *individual style*. That's what I think is cool.

2 Grace
I love cool things of all kinds. You can find lots of *great things* in second-hand shops. You know, some things are so uncool that *they're cool*!

3 Ryan
In my school there's a lot of *peer pressure* to be cool and fashionable. That's not a good thing, in my opinion. I think you should *just be yourself*.

4 Ananya
I think a lot of people want to be cool so that other people will *like them*. I think that's a pity. People should like you for who you are. You shouldn't care what *other people think*.

5 Nathan
To be cool, you have to wear the right clothes and like *the right music*.

6 Ella
I think it's really cool to have lots of piercings and tattoos. They make you look *really interesting*.

7 Adam
I don't want to be the same as everybody else. I think it's cool to *be different*!

b) Do you agree with these people? What do you think? Write in your exercise book.

> I agree very much / quite a lot / a bit with … (Lucy/Grace/…)
> I totally disagree with …
> In my opinion • I think

▶ SB p. 75

forty-seven 47

4 THEMES

2 Being a screenager
Change the words in orange. Find words and phrases in the box that mean the same thing.

> all over the world • at the same time • chat • focus on • get information •
> multitask • online • pros and cons • text • ~~the average~~ • they're addicted

The average
~~A typical~~ teenager in the USA spends over eight hours a day in front of the screen. And they're not just doing one thing: most of the time they do lots of things [*multitask*]. They might talk [*chat*] with a friend on a social media site, send text messages to [*text*] other friends, and play a video game, all together [*at the same time*].

What are the advantages and disadvantages [*pros and cons*] of digital technology?

Well, you can find out about things [*get information*] very quickly, and you can communicate with people in lots of different countries [*all over the world*]. But there are downsides. Young people often can't concentrate[1] [*focus on*] on their homework. And they don't get enough sleep because they're on the internet [*online*] at night. Some teenagers just can't stop – it's like a drug [*they're addicted*]!

▶ SB p. 77

3 Your phone and you
More help p. 80

a) How many different things do you use your phone for? Make a list in your exercise book, e.g.:

I use my phone to go online, video-chat...

b) Compare with a partner. Do you use your phone for the same things? What do you use it for most?

▶ SB p. 77

4 SPEAKING Technology then and now
More help p. 80

! Take turns to read the questions.

Think about when your parents and teachers were young.
Discuss the answers to these questions with a partner. Give your opinion too.

1. How do you think they listened to music?
2. How did they watch films?
3. How did they communicate with their friends?
4. How did they spend their free time?
5. Was this very different from today? How?
6. What were their mobile phones like?
7. Did they have smart phones?
8. What were their computers like?
9. Did they use the internet as much as you?
10. Did they have as much technology as you?

▶ SB p. 77

[1] concentrate *sich konzentrieren*

48 forty-eight

THEMES 4

5 LISTENING Profile pictures

What is each person's profile picture? Write notes in the grid.

> **You hear:** a picture of...
> me (on a horse)
> my (dog)
>
> **You write:** a picture of...
> ▸ him / **her** (on a horse)
> ▸ **his** / her (dog)

Person	Profile picture is a picture of...
1 Ella	her baby brother
2 Alexander	him on his bike
3 Natasha	her and her boyfriend
4 Lewis	a black horse
5 Mohammed	his eyes and the top of his head
6 Anna	her band

▸ SB p. 78

6 MEDIATION Has social media gone too far?

Read the joke and explain it in German for a friend.

> You don't have to translate every word.

Before social media, did you...

take a photo of your dinner...

run into town to get lots of copies

then give them to your family and friends, and to all their friends?

▸ SB p. 79

7 SPEAKING Ads on the internet

What do you think of ads on the internet? What are the pros and cons? What kinds of ads do you like? Discuss with a partner.

Well, on the one hand,...

Ideas:
A lot of / some ads are...
I like / hate ads that are...
 funny • cute • creative • imaginative • strange •
 cool • a pain • irritating • stupid • crazy.
Ads keep websites free / are useful.
When there are ads, I can't focus on the website.
I don't mind ads.

▸ SB p. 79

forty-nine 49

4 THEMES

8 READING A new band

a) ⊙ Skim the article and choose a good title for it:

> **Skimming:** Look through the text quickly. You don't have to read *every* word.

a) Starting a band ☐   b) Marketing your band ✓   c) Making your first CD ☐

Let people hear the music!

The first thing is: you have to get your music out there – people have to hear it! Play as many live gigs[1] as you can, for example organise gigs in bars and at music festivals. You can play at school concerts and even at people's birthday parties. Look out for competitions for new bands, and don't forget charity events. Even if you don't get paid, playing live is a great way to advertise. Another idea is to ask a shop in your High Street if you can play live there – a music store or a cool clothes shop. They get extra customers, and you get to play to new people. And don't forget to advertise your gigs. Put up posters and flyers at least a week before the gig.

Go online

Nothing happens these days without the internet. All bands need a good website with information about the band, lots of photos and personal information about band members. And of course don't forget social media sites. Make your profiles as interesting as possible. Keep the information fresh, and have a list of gigs you're going to play. It's a good idea to have a blog too. And most importantly, put videos of your songs on music sites so that more people can hear them.

It's who you know…

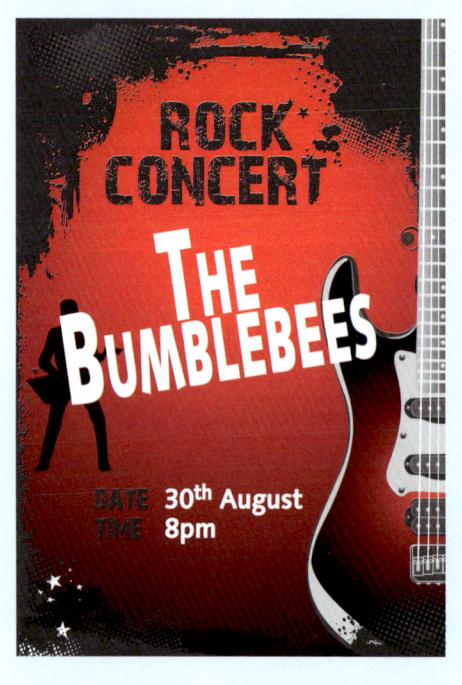

Talk to lots of people! Go to other bands' gigs, and talk to them, and to people in their audience. You don't know who you might meet! Be friendly to your fans – chat to them after gigs, and if they write comments or your web pages, always answer them. Happy fans will tell their friends about you. Contact music writers too: send them information about your band, and a link to a free download.

Things to give and sell

You need 'merch': things for people to buy at your gigs, for example T-shirts and sweatshirts. Girls like to buy bags. And of course, you must have CDs to sell. Make sure your band's name is in big letters, and if someone can design a great logo for you, even better! Have things you can give away free to fans too, like postcards, badges, pens, etc.

But the most important thing is: keep practising and be an awesome band!!

[1] gig *Konzert*

THEMES 4

b) Answer these questions about the article.

> To help you, first find and highlight the answers in the text.

1 The article gives ideas for where a band can play live. Write down **seven** places.
bars, music festivals, school concert, birthday parties, competitions, charity events, a shop in the High Street

2 Find **four** ways in the article to use the internet for marketing a band.
website, social media sites, blog, videos on music sites

3 Note **four** groups of people who the article says bands should talk to or contact.
other bands, people in their audience, fans, music writers

4 Write down **four** things it suggests that bands should sell, and three things to give away free.
sell: T-shirts, sweatshirts, bags, CDs
give away: postcars, badges, pens

c) True, false or not in the text?

True / False / Not in text

1 It's best to put up posters two days before a concert. — False
2 Emails can be useful for advertising gigs. — Not in text
3 It's good to put information about concerts on the internet — True
4 Never let people listen to your songs for free. — False
5 Your manager can help you get good gigs. — Not in text
6 Don't have a logo – it isn't cool. — False

▶ SB p. 81

Manager of a band   More help p. 80

A new band are playing their first gig in two months' time. What does their manager need to do? Make a list of things to do in your exercise book.

Make posters for the concert.
Put up the posters. *(where? when?)*

> You can get ideas from the article on p. 50.

▶ SB p. 81

fifty-one 51

4 FOCUS ON LANGUAGE

10 Last summer could have been better…

a) Ananya writes about her holiday. Make sentences by drawing lines.

1 If I had put sun cream on, … — my arms wouldn't have been so red.
2 If I hadn't left my phone at home, … — I would have texted my friends.
3 If I had taken more money, … — I would have gone on a boat trip.
4 If I hadn't forgotten my ball, … — we would have played football.
5 If I had gone to bed earlier, … — I wouldn't have felt so tired all the time.
6 If I hadn't eaten too much ice-cream, … — I wouldn't have had stomach ache.

b) Lewis writes about his holiday. Write the correct forms of the verbs.

1 If we _had travelled_ (travel) by plane, we would have got there faster.
2 If I _hadn't been_ (not be) so scared, I would have done a bungee jump.
3 If we _had had_ (have) more money, we would have gone on a boat trip.
4 If we had had more time, we _would have done_ (do) more things.
5 If I had taken your address with me, I _would have sent_ (send) you a post card.
6 If we had known how bad the hotel was, we _wouldn't have gone_ (not go) there.

c) Natasha's holiday. Write the correct forms of the verbs.

1 If it _had been_ (be) sunny, we _would have gone_ (go) to the beach.
2 If it _hadn't rained_ (not rain) so much, I _would have enjoyed_ (enjoy) the holiday much more.
3 If Dad _had checked_ (check) the timetable, we _wouldn't have missed_ (not miss) the ferry.
4 If we _had taken_ (take) a map, we _wouldn't have got_ (get) lost.
5 If we _had visited_ (visit) our friends in Germany, I _would have spoken_ (spoken) German with them.
6 If I _had chosen_ (choose) our holiday, it _would have been_ (be) more fun.

More challenge 4 | p. 81
▶ SB p. 83

FOCUS ON LANGUAGE   4

11 REVISION Messages
Lewis and Anna are sending messages to each other.
Circle the correct forms of the adjectives and adverbs.

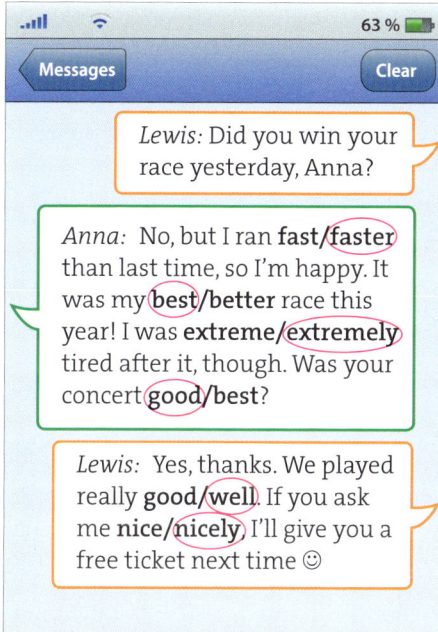

Lewis: Did you win your race yesterday, Anna?

Anna: No, but I ran **fast**/**faster** than last time, so I'm happy. It was my **best**/**better** race this year! I was **extreme**/**extremely** tired after it, though. Was your concert **good**/**best**?

Lewis: Yes, thanks. We played really **good**/**well**. If you ask me **nice**/**nicely** I'll give you a free ticket next time ☺

12 REVISION Advice from friends
Nathan asks his friends a question on a social media site.
Read the text, then tick (✓) the correct options below.

Nathan   I'm thinking of getting a tattoo. What do you **1**?

Ryan   No, **2** do it, Nathan! In two years' time you might not like it. Think about it for a few months first, then you can decide.

Grace   I think you should **3** a tattoo. They're really cool.

Jimi   I got a tattoo three months **4**. I love it, but when my mum saw it, she **5** crazy! ☹

Ella   You can't, Nathan. You **6** be 18 for a tattoo in the UK. Sorry – **7** too young.

Nathan   Thanks, guys. It looks like I'll have to wait **8** I'm 18, and decide then.

1 thought ☐   think ✓   thinks ☐   thinking ☐
2 don't ✓   can't ☐   won't ☐   didn't ☐
3 become ☐   take ☐   get ✓   buy ☐
4 for ☐   ago ✓   before ☐   away ☐
5 go ☐   going ☐   goes ☐   went ✓
6 will ☐   needn't ☐   have to ✓   can ☐
7 yours ☐   you're ✓   you ☐   your ☐
8 before ☐   while ☐   when ☐   until ✓

fifty-three 53

4 FOCUS ON LANGUAGE

13 REVISION Last weekend
Read what the four friends say about the weekend.
Complete the sentences with at/in/to.

I did a lot _at_ the weekend. I took part _in_ a singing competition. I was really nervous, singing _in_ front of hundreds of people. Then on Sunday I went _to_ London for the day.

I went _to_ a party on Saturday, then I spent Sunday _at_ Anna's house. I met a nice boy _at_ the party. He works _in_ an office in town.

I spent the weekend _in_ the country. _In_ my opinion, it's better than being the city! Nobody is _in_ a hurry – you can relax and chill. We're going back _at_ Christmas.

I didn't feel well on Sunday, so I stayed _at_ home – and went _to_ sleep on the sofa _at_ 4 o'clock! I just went _to_ bed in the evening. _At_ the moment, I still don't feel good, so I might not go _to_ school tomorrow.

14 REVISION Ananya's weekend
Ananya is talking about her weekend. Complete her sentences with suitable[1] words.

1 I _spent_ the weekend with my aunt and cousins.
2 We get on well together, so I had a _great_ time.
3 On Saturday, we _played_ tennis in the park.
4 I didn't win any games – my cousins are _better_ than me.
5 In the evening, we went to the cinema. The film was funny, and I _enjoyed_ it very much.
6 We wanted to go on a picnic on Sunday, but the weather was _bad_, so we stayed in the house.
7 My cousins invited some _friends_ and we played cards.
8 I came _back_ by train in on Sunday evening.

[1] suitable *passend*

TEXT 4

15 New words quiz
a) Find these new words from the story.

1. two people born at the same time to the same mum
2. If you have a lot of money, you're ...
3. go towards someone very quietly
4. Don't come near me. = Leave me ...
5. let something fall from your hands
6. If something isn't real but it looks real, it's ...
7. This very, very small thing can make you ill.

8. It moves, it doesn't stay in one place. It's ...
9. the streets behind the main street
10. a very stupid person
11. This is on top of a building.
12. You might go up this to wash a high window.

T	W	I	N	S				
R	I	C	H					
C	R	E	E	P		U	P	
A	L	O	N	E				
D	R	O	P					
R	E	A	L	I	S	T	I	C
V	I	R	U	S				
M	O	B	I	L	E			
B	A	C	K	S	T	R	E	E	T	S
I	D	I	O	T				
R	O	O	F					
L	A	D	D	E	R			

b) Put the letters in **yellow** into the right order. It's the name of the computer game in the story.

Virtual Kombat ▶ SB p. 87

16 What would you have done?
If you had been Scott, what would you have done? Write six sentences.

I would have	fought the two bullies • been afraid
I wouldn't have	run away from Shark • eaten the children's bread •
	joined Shark's gang • taken Tommy's place

▶ SB p. 87

17 Everyone has a story. More help p. 82
Choose Shark, Tommy or Tammy. Imagine his/her story. Write in your exercise book.

Ideas:
How old was he/she when his/her parents died?
Where did the family live before?
What was their life like before?
What does this character think of the other people in the story?
What does he/she hope will happen in the future?

▶ SB p. 87

fifty-five 55

4 SKILLS

A

Mobile phones

People today can't imagine life without a mobile phone. In fact about 75 % of people in the world use a mobile phone. But actually, the mobile is quite a recent invention.

The first call
The very first mobile phone call was made on 3rd April 1973 by Martin Cooper, who was an engineer and inventor[1] at Motorola in the USA. Who did he phone? His wife? The president? No, he phoned another telephone company, to show them that Motorola had got there first! The giant phone measured 22.8 x 12.7 x 4.4 cm and weighed no less than 1.1 kg.

A phone to buy
The first mobile phone was sold in shops ten years later, in 1983. This was the Motorola DynaTAC 8000X. It had 30 minutes of talk time, and took about ten hours to charge[2]. It measured 30 x 8.9 x 4.4 cm and weighed 794 g. And it wasn't cheap, at a price of $3,995. However, in spite of the price, it was very popular and there was even a waiting list of six months.

Time to text
The early nineties was an important time in mobile phone history. In 1991, Second Generation (2G) phones were developed in Finland, making SMS text messages possible. The first text message was sent from a computer to a mobile phone via the Vodafone network in the UK on 3rd December 1992. The message read "Happy Christmas".

Smile, please!
In 1997, Philippe Kahn, a French-born technology inventor, put together a camera and a mobile phone, and sent the first photos by phone. They were pictures of his new baby daughter, sent from the hospital to more than 2000 people. The first commercial camera phones, made by Samsung and Sharp, were in shops in South Korea and Japan in 2000.

B

Five phone facts

★ The computer in your smartphone is better than the computers they used to send Apollo 11 astronauts to the moon in 1969.
★ In Britain, 100,000 mobile phones are dropped into the toilet every year.
★ 90 – 95% of mobile phones in Japan are waterproof – water will not damage them. That's because Japanese teenagers love their mobiles so much, they even use them in the shower or bath.
★ More people in the world have mobile phones than toilets.
★ 70 % of mobile phones are made in China.

[1] inventor *Erfinder*   [2] charge *aufladen*

SKILLS   4

18 ⭕ **READING** What are the articles about?
Skim through the two articles quickly. Which phrases best describe the articles?

Article A = _3_
Article B = _2_

1. The best mobile phone you can buy.
2. Some interesting things about mobile phones.
3. A history of mobile phones.
4. How to use a smartphone.

19 **READING** Information from the articles
a) Read the first article. Tick (✓) the right answers.

> ❗ You won't always find the same words in the text as in the questions. Look for words and phrases that mean the same.

1. How many people use a mobile phone?
   a) Half (1/2) of the world's population. ☐
   b) Two thirds (2/3) of the world's population. ☐
   c) Three quarters (3/4) of the world's population. ✓

2. Martin Cooper made the first mobile phone call. Who did he talk to?
   a) An inventor at the Motorola company. ☐
   b) Another phone company. ✓
   c) The President of the USA. ☐

3. In what year could people first buy a mobile phone?
   a) In 1973. ☐
   b) In 1983. ✓
   c) In 1991. ☐

4. How long could they talk on the phone for, before they had to charge it?
   a) Half an hour. ✓
   b) Three hours. ☐
   c) Ten hours. ☐

5. How much did the first mobile phone cost to buy?
   a) Nearly forty dollars. ☐
   b) Nearly one thousand dollars. ☐
   c) Nearly four thousand dollars. ✓

6. In the early 1990s, you could use your mobile phone to
   a) text people. ✓
   b) send photos. ☐
   c) go on the internet. ☐

b) Read the second article. Tick (✓) the right answers.

	True	False	Not in text
1 You can drop most Japanese mobiles into water without a problem.	✓		
2 The most common use of a mobile is to check the time.			✓
3 Japan makes more mobile phones than China.		✓	

fifty-seven **57**

4 SKILLS

20 LISTENING Find the information.

a) Listen and fill in the information.

1. Steve Wozniak wanted a phone number where the numbers were all _the same_.
2. His new number was _888 – 8888_.
3. But he had a problem: he got _more than 100_ phone calls every day.
4. In the end, Steve understood: the phone calls were from _babies!_
5. There was only one thing to do: he _changed his number._

b) What do you think would have happened if Steve had had the number 777-7777?

I think he would still have got phone calls from babies.

---

21 WRITING Phones and selfies

Choose task A or B.
Don't do both tasks.

Task A Tell the story behind this picture.
○ Write about 100 words.
● Write about 150 words.

Write about:
- who these people are and how they know each other,
- where they are,
- what they are doing,
- and what you think will happen next.

> Think what tenses will be useful.
> They've come here because…
> They're having a good time.
> They'll probably go…

Task B "Mobile phones are terrible for teenagers!"
Give reasons for and against this statement, and give your own opinion.
○ Write about 100 words.
● Write about 150 words.

> Don't forget useful phrases for giving your opinion, e.g.
> on the one hand; on the other hand; however, I disagree.

> Remember to:
> - structure and plan your text.
> - choose words and phrases carefully, so the text will flow well and the reader will be impressed by your English!
> - check your work when you've finished.

Sample answers p. 70

MY LEARNER LOG

Das habe ich in Unit 4 gelernt:			
Ich kann …	Hier habe ich's gelernt/geübt:	Und wie gut bin ich darin wirklich? Selbsteinschätzung oder Lehrereinschätzung:	Frage deine Lehrerin oder deinen Lehrer nun nach passendem Übungsmaterial:
… einen Podcast hören und ihm Informationen entnehmen.	S. 74, 77 Stop! Check! Go! 4	☺ 😐 ☹	DFF 4.1 DFF 4.1 DFF 4.1
… einem Artikel Informationen entnehmen.	S. 76–77, 80–81, 82–83 Stop! Check! Go! 3	☺ 😐 ☹	DFF 4.2 DFF 4.2 DFF 4.2
… ein Bild beschreiben und über dessen Inhalte sprechen.	S. 77, 97 Stop! Check! Go! 6	☺ 😐 ☹	DFF 4.3 DFF 4.3 DFF 4.3
… über *social media* schreiben.	S. 79 Stop! Check! Go! 5	☺ 😐 ☹	DFF 4.4 DFF 4.4 DFF 4.4
… wichtige Informationen aus dem Englischen ins Deutsche übertragen.	S. 81 Stop! Check! Go! 7	☺ 😐 ☹	DFF 4.5 DFF 4.5 DFF 4.5
… sagen „was gewesen wäre, wenn …" (conditional sentences type 3).	S. 82–83 Stop! Check! Go! 2	☺ 😐 ☹	DFF 4.6 DFF 4.6 DFF 4.6
… Begriffe zum Wortfeld *technology and social media* anwenden.	S. 74–84 Stop! Check! Go! 1	☺ 😐 ☹	DFF 4.7 DFF 4.7 DFF 4.7
… ein Graffiti beschreiben und darüber sprechen.	S. 94	☺ 😐 ☹	DFF 4.8 DFF 4.8 DFF 4.8

Du kannst diese Seite auch in dein Dossier heften, wenn du fertig bist.

fifty-nine

4 REVISION

1 A trip to our aunt and uncle's house
Circle the right pronouns in the text.

My brother and I went to stay with us /(our)/ her aunt and uncle and (their)/ them / they four cats. My uncle took (me)/ I / my and my brother to him / her /(his) favourite cafe and we had ice-creams. A friend of my uncle's saw he /(him)/ her and she came over and sat with we /(us)/ our. She's a singer and gave us tickets for his /(her)/ she next concert! My aunt and uncle are really nice. We're going to stay with they /(them)/ their again in the summer.

2 Asking for help
Complete the conversation with the missing words. You won't need all the words in the box.

> cost • every • help • here • hope • last • nearly •
> per • price • tickets • time • welcome • wonder

Tourist   I *wonder* if you could help me. What *time* are the bus tours, please?

Assistant   Sure! They're *every* half hour from 10 am until 6 pm.

Tourist   How long does a tour *last*?

Assistant   *Nearly* two hours: about one hour fifty-five.

Tourist   Thank you. And how much does a tour *cost*?

Assistant   Fifty-two dollars *per* person.

Tourist   Thanks. I'd like three *tickets*, please.

Assistant   *Here* you are.

Tourist   Thanks for your *help*.

Assistant   You're *welcome*. Have a nice day.

3 Tourists in New York – and in your town
Your Australian penfriend, Kai, asks about New York – and a town near you.
Write an email and answer his questions.

- If you went to New York, what would you do there?
- Would you like to visit New York? Why / Why not?
- Do lots of tourists visit your town? Why / Why not?
- Where can tourists get information about the town?

! Look on the internet for ideas if you need to.

! Compare with a partner – do you agree with what he / she has written?

EXAM PREPARATION

1 LISTENING Declan's birthday

13 Listen to four conversations.
For each question tick (✓) the correct answer: A, B or C.
You can listen twice.

> Students who are getting ready for exams at the end of year 9 will find extra practice here.

1 What did Declan do on his birthday?

A B  ✓ C

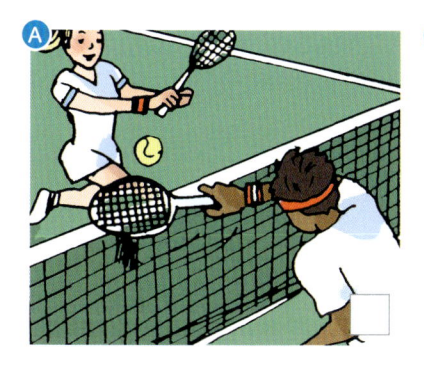

2 What did Declan do in the evening?

A ✓ B  C

3 What present did Uncle John give Declan?

A B  C ✓

> You won't always hear the exact answer. You might have to think about it!

4 At what time will Samira go to Declan's house?

A 6 o'clock   B 7 o'clock ✓   C 8 o'clock

sixty-one 61

EXAM PREPARATION

🎧 **2 LISTENING Samira's terrible day**
14 Samira is telling Declan about her terrible day. Read the sentences and tick (✓) true or false. You can listen twice.

> Read the sentences before you listen so that you know what information you're looking for.

> You won't hear the same words that you read in the sentences.

True / False

1 Samira went to school by bike because the car was at the garage. ☐ ✓
2 The weather was wet this morning. ✓ ☐
3 Samira had an accident on her bike. ✓ ☐
4 She didn't get hurt. ☐ ✓
5 Samira's bike was broken. ☐ ✓
6 Samira did badly in a maths test. ☐ ✓

🎧 **3 LISTENING A phone message**
15 Samira's mum, Mrs Khan, has a voicemail message. Listen and write the missing information. You can listen twice.

> If you have to write down numbers or letters, say them in your head to help you remember them.

1 The message is from: *the garage*
2 Car number: *KH65GCW*
3 A problem with: *the engine*
4 What they need to do: *order a new part*
5 Garage phone number: *724 691*
6 The car will be ready: *end of the week*

ENGLISH G LIGHTHOUSE

Materialien zu Band 5

Cornelsen

Die folgenden Titel können Sie über Ihren Buchhändler beziehen und Ihren örtlichen Buchhandel unterstützen.

Sie können die Titel auch direkt bei uns ordern. Bestellen Sie in diesem Fall einfach über unsere Website (zzgl. einer Versandkostenpauschale von 2,95 € pro Sendung): www.cornelsen.de/lighthouse-eltern

Alles für den **sicheren Lernerfolg** Ihres Kindes

Anzahl

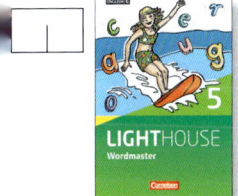

Wordmaster – Vokabellernbuch
Abwechslungsreiches und spielerisches Üben und Schreiben der neuen Vokabeln in immer wieder anderen Zusammenhängen – ein modernes Vokabeltrainingsheft.
978-3-06-032385-2   7,75 €

Anzahl

Klassenarbeitstrainer mit Lösungen und Audios online
Zwei Muster-Klassenarbeiten zu jeder Unit, mit denen Lese- und Hörverstehen, Schreiben sowie praktischer Sprachgebrauch trainiert werden können.
978-3-06-032383-8   10,25 €

Vokabeltaschenbuch
Das Vokabular des Buches im praktischen Kleinformat für unterwegs.
978-3-06-033998-3   5,25 €

Abgestimmt auf *English G Lighthouse*, Band 5

Lektüre „Riot"
Der Norden Londons gerät außer Kontrolle. *Riot* erzählt die Geschichte von Danny, einem 15-jährigen Jungen aus Tottenham, der in den Strudel dieser Ereignisse gerät. Ein Auszug dieses Jugendromans ist im *Textfile* von *English G Lighthouse* 5 enthalten.
978-3-06-033180-2   8,99 €

Außerdem erhältlich:

Vokabeltrainer-App
Vokabeln üben, Tests und Prüfungen auf dem Smartphone – passend zu *English G Lighthouse*. Kostenlos im Store herunterladen und den passenden Wortschatz direkt in der Vokabeltrainer-App kaufen.

Vokabelpaket zu Band 5   ◇   5,99 €

Infos unter www.cornelsen.de/vokabeltrainer oder einfach QR-Code scannen.

Zeichenerklärung: ◇ Unverbindliche Preisempfehlung   Preise Stand 1.1.2016

Infos rund um *English G Lighthouse* für Sie und Ihr Kind: **www.cornelsen.de/lighthouse-eltern**

EXAM PREPARATION

4 READING An article in a school magazine

Our school exchange

Last October was our first exchange visit to Germany, and this year in the May half-term holiday, we welcomed our exchange partners from Germany for the first time. They stayed with our students and their families and very much enjoyed their experience of British life.

On some of the days, our guests were with their British exchange partners and their families, but on other days, we met up as one big group and did things together. One of the highlights was the trip to Ilfracombe. Everyone enjoyed having fish and chips down at the harbour – a typical British seaside lunch. The seagulls would have had some too, if we had let them!

In the afternoon, half of the group went to the Aquarium and the other half went on a boat trip and saw lots of sea birds and some seals. Fortunately, no-one was seasick!

Everyone took lots of great photos during the exchange, and we have put them up on the school website. We are already planning a trip to Germany next spring and we hope that our school exchange will go on for many years to come.

a) Correct the mistakes in these sentences. The correct information is in the text.

1 The German students came to the British school in October.
   Correct: *May*

2 This was the Germans' second visit to the British school.
   Correct: *first*

3 The German students did things with their British families every day
   Correct: *on some of the days*

4 They had pizza for lunch in Ilfracombe.
   Correct: *fish and chips*

> **Remember to:**
> - Sentences are usually in the same order as the text.
> - The sentences don't use exactly the same words as in the text. To find the right information, look for key words in the text, and read what comes before and after.

b) Are these sentences **true**, **false** or is the information **not in the text**?

	True	False	Not in text
1 After lunch, the whole group went on a boat trip.		✓	
2 Students saw sea birds from the boat.	✓		
3 The boat trip was very expensive.			✓
4 There are plans for an exchange trip next year.	✓		

EXAM PREPARATION

5 READING Saving lives at sea

The town of Ilfracombe in Devon, south-west England, has had a lifeboat[1] station for nearly 180 years. At the moment, the station has two lifeboats, which are run by the RNLI.

The RNLI (Royal National Lifeboat Institution), a famous organisation in Britain, is a charity that saves lives at sea. The organisation was founded in 1824, and since then it has saved more than 140,000 people's lives and has helped thousands more people to get back to dry land from the sea.

Around the UK and Ireland there are 237 RNLI lifeboat stations, with a total of 346 lifeboats. There are 4,600 lifeboat crew members – and most of them are volunteers. Most of them have other jobs, for example, there are teachers, office workers, garage mechanics and university students. When they are called to help, these people must stop what they're doing and go to the lifeboat station as fast as possible, day or night.

The biggest rescue in the RNLI's history was on 17 March 1907 when a huge ship hit rocks off the coast of Cornwall. Fighting through stormy winds and fog, RNLI lifeboats worked for sixteen hours and rescued 456 people, including 70 babies.

These RNLI volunteers are brave people. Their work is dangerous, and they risk their own lives to help other people.

Read the text. Then write the answers to the questions.
Do not write sentences. Write numbers, words or notes only.

> Always read the instructions carefully. Check if you need to answer in sentences or not.

1 How long has there been a lifeboat station in Ilfracombe?
   nearly 180 years

2 What does the RNLI do?
   saves lives at sea

3 How many lives has it saved since it began?
   more than 140,000

4 How many boats does the RNLI have?
   346

> Remember! The words in the question aren't always exactly the same as the words in the text.

5 How much money do most RNLI workers get for rescuing people?
   nothing

6 Describe the weather on the day of the RNLI's biggest rescue.
   stormy winds and fog

[1] lifeboat *Rettungsboot*

EXAM PREPARATION

6 LANGUAGE A tour with a difference
Read the text. Tick (✓) the correct word.

1. who ☐ when ☐ what ✓ which ☐
2. must ☐ can ✓ often ☐ always ☐
3. most ☐ main ✓ high ☐ top ☐
4. took ☐ takes ☐ taking ☐ take ✓
5. most ✓ more ☐ best ☐ better ☐
6. as ☐ and ☐ too ☐ also ✓
7. so ☐ as ☐ like ✓ why ☐

> When you've chosen a word, read the whole sentence. Is it right?

You've heard of *bus* tours... but ① is a *Rebus* tour? Well, it's a type of tour you ② go on in Edinburgh. Detective Inspector John Rebus is the ③ character in the crime novels of Scottish writer Ian Rankin. Rebus works in Edinburgh, and the tours ④ fans to some of the places in the books. These aren't typical tourist places. They aren't the ⑤ beautiful areas of Edinburgh but many of them show the dark and secret sides of the city and its history. You visit places that are found in the novels but you ⑥ learn about Edinburgh's past and some of the famous people who lived there. A walking tour ⑦ this is a great way to get to know this interesting city.

7 LANGUAGE Hobbies
Samira is writing an email to her German exchange partner. Complete her sentences with one, two or three suitable[1] words.

> Read the *whole* sentence and think about what word could be right. Remember to think about the spelling.

Hi Jonas!

In your last email you _asked_ me if I liked reading. Yes, _I do_! I usually read about two or three books _every_ week. My favourite books are crime novels. I love them because they're so _exciting_. _What sort of_ books do you like? I like _watching_ crime series on TV too. _What_ about you? What are your favourite programmes? _Are there_ any British crime programmes on German TV? Have you _ever_ read any crime novels by British writers?

---

[1] suitable *geeignet*

sixty-five 65

EXAM PREPARATION

8 WRITING Your town

You got this email from your British exchange partner, Johnny.

> Read the instructions carefully. Make sure you give all the information.
> How many questions are there in this exercise? Answer all of them.

Write an email to Johnny and answer his questions.
Write 60–80 words.

Hi there!

I'm looking forward to coming to your town on the school exchange.

I wanted to ask you about your town. What is it like?
What is there for young people to do in the town? And what is there for tourists?

I want to buy lots of presents for my family! Where can I go shopping in town?

I've never been to Germany before. I can't wait to come!

Bye for now
Johnny

> If you don't know a word, say it another way, or say something different.
> For example, you've forgotten the words in blue. How can you say it differently?
>
> 1 My town is huge. ▸ My town is *very big*.
> 2 The town centre is very busy. ▸ There are *lots of people* in the town centre.
> 3 There's a swimming pool. ▸ You can *go swimming*.

_____
_____
_____
_____
_____
_____

> Check your work when you've finished.
> ✓ Have you answered all the questions?
> ✓ Is the spelling right?
> ✓ And the verbs?
> ✓ Have you used adjectives (e.g. great) and qualifiers (e.g. quite)

> Count[1] the words.
> ✓ Have you written enough?

[1] count *zählen*

sixty-six

EXAM PREPARATION

9 MEDIATION Asking the way

You are visiting your cousin Leonie in Zurich. A British tourist asks for some help. Leonie can't speak English and the tourist can't speak German! Help them.

> ! If you can't remember a word, don't write nothing! Say it another way, or say something that means nearly the same.
>
> | If you've forgotten… | you could say: |
> |---|---|
> | next to | very near |
> | on foot | if you walk |

Tourist	Excuse me. Is the FIFA Museum near here?
You	*Er möchte wissen, ob das FIFA-Museum in der Nähe ist.*
Leonie	Es ist in der Seestraße, in der Nähe von der Kirche.
You	*It's on Seestraße, near the church.*
Tourist	Thanks a lot. Is it far?
You	*Danke sehr. Ist es weit?*
Leonie	Nein, es sind zehn Minuten zu Fuß.
You	*No, it's only ten minutes on foot.*
Tourist	How do I get there?
You	*Wie kommt er dahin?*
Leonie	Gehen Sie diese Straße entlang und dann bei der Post rechts abbiegen.
You	*Go along this street then turn right at the post office.*
Tourist	Is the museum open today?
You	*Hat das Museum heute auf?*
Leonie	Ja. Es hat jeden Tag außer montags auf.
You	*Yes. It's open every day except Mondays.*
Tourist	And can I get something to eat there?
You	*Kann er dort etwas zum Essen bekommen?*
Leonie	Ja. Es gibt im Erdgeschoß ein Cafe.
You	*Yes. There's a cafe on the ground floor.*
Leonie	Viel Spaß im Museum!
You	*Enjoy the museum!*

EXAM PREPARATION

10 SPEAKING Talking about a picture – PARTNER A
(PARTNER B: Go to p. 84)
Talk to your partner for two minutes.

- What can you see in the picture?
- Who are the people and what are they saying?
- What is your bedroom like?
- What do you like doing in your room?

> ! Say more than the minimum. Show how good your English is!
>
> There are two girls. ▶ There are two girls. One girl is writing in a book and the other girl is using a computer.

11 SPEAKING Role plays – PARTNER A
(PARTNER B: Go to p. 84)

> ! Read all the things on the card before you start. Think about how to make complete sentences. Remember to say *please* and *thank you*.

1
You phone your friend Nathan. His sister answers the phone.

- speak to Nathan?
- message?
- I have tickets for concert
- Friday / 7.30
- thank / phone this evening?

2
Your friend suggests something to do at the weekend.

- yes
- no – party
- where meet? / time?
- where / sports centre?
- great / see then

68 sixty-eight

SAMPLE ANSWERS

Unit 1

25 A holiday

Last year I went on holiday to Spain with my family. We stayed in a nice apartment near the beach, and the sun shone every day. I had an absolutely awesome time!

The best part was the day we went on a boat trip. The boat was quite big and there were three other families on board. In the morning, we went fishing from the boat. I didn't catch any fish, but I didn't mind because it was great fun. Then at lunchtime we got off the boat and we all had a big barbecue on a beautiful sandy beach.

After lunch, we played on the beach and went snorkelling. I'd never been snorkelling before, but it was quite easy. Then we came back on the boat.

I really enjoyed the holiday, and I hope we'll go back to the same place next year. Maybe we'll meet those other families again too.

Unit 2

21 Asking for something

Dialogue 1	Dialogue 2
– Mum, can I talk to you about weekend, please? – Yes, of course. – There's a party at Tim's house. Is it OK if I stay until one o'clock? – One o'clock? No, that's too late. – Is 12.30 OK? – That's still very late. – I know you worry about me when I come home late, but I can get the bus with Katie and Harry. – I don't know… OK, you can stay until midnight, and I'll pick you up in the car. – Great, Mum. Thanks!	– Mum, can I have some more pocket money and can I go to a concert on Friday night? – Not now. Can't you see I'm busy? – Dad, can I have some more pocket money? – No, not this week. – But dad, I need new jeans and I want to buy a ticket for a concert. – I said no. – Dad! That's not fair! All my friends are going to the concert. – For the last time – no! – You never give me anything! You don't care!

3-4 SAMPLE ANSWERS

Unit 3

25 Writing about a job

Task 1:
I had a Saturday job in a shoe shop. I'd never worked in a shop before, but my first day went very well. First, I was introduced to the other shop assistants. I didn't feel too nervous, because everyone was so friendly. Then the manager explained everything to me and told me to watch the others. I had to listen to what they said to the customers.

At lunchtime, I went to the cafe next door with two assistants from the shop. They said that they enjoyed working there, but the shop wasn't making enough money.

After lunch, I was allowed to serve my first customer. She looked rich and she was wearing expensive clothes. I showed her lots of shoes, and in the end she bought seven pairs of expensive shoes! I couldn't believe it! The manager was extremely pleased and gave me some extra money. What a great first day!

Task 2:
The interesting job I'd like to write about is being an acrobat in a circus. Acrobats are great, because they have a lot of skills and their performance is glamorous.

Of course, you have to work really hard and do a lot of training. You travel a lot with the circus too. I think that's a positive and a negative thing. It's interesting to see new places, but you don't see your family for a long time. However, you live with your friends in the circus.

I don't know what the working hours are, but I think they're long. You have to perform every night. You probably don't earn a lot of money, but you don't need to buy a house.

I'd love to be an acrobat, because I think it would be fun and exciting. I've been to the circus more than ten times, and it's always a fantastic show.

Unit 4

21 Phones and selfies

Task A:
This is a group of young people who all work together in an office. They've known each other for more than a year, and they're good friends.

They live near the mountains and there is a lot of snow this year. Today it's Saturday and they drove to the mountains this morning in their cars. There is a shop where you can hire sports equipment and these friends have got inflatable seats so that they can slide down the mountain. They're having a great time. Everyone is feeling very happy because it's Saturday and they don't have to work. There aren't many people there and it isn't too cold. At the moment, they're taking a selfie of the group and I think they'll put it on their social media pages.

I think the young people will probably stay in the mountains till evening, then they'll go home.

Task B:
Some adults say that mobile phones are terrible for teenagers. There are a few reasons for this.

It's true that some teenagers spend too much time on their phones. For example, some people are always tired because they surf the net when they're in bed and don't sleep enough. Many students can't focus on their homework because they're texting their friends at the same time. Some parents think teenagers shouldn't have mobiles.

However, I disagree. One the one hand, some people use their phones too much. But on the other hand, mobiles are very useful. You can phone your parents if you've missed the bus, for example. They can also help you with your homework, because you can find information on the internet. And it's easy to chat with friends who are far away.

To sum up, there are pros and cons – but I think mobile phones can be great for teenagers.

DIFF BANK

Unit 1

More help **2** New words

b) Find a different way to say the same thing in English.
The words after the sentences will help you.

1 Smoking is **banned** in restaurants. _Smoking isn't allowed_ in restaurants. (not allowed)

2 **Central** Australia is flat. _The middle of Australia_ is flat. (middle of)

3 **One in ten** visitors is from China. – _10% of visitors_ are from China. (10 %)

4 Native animals will **suffer**. Life will _get worse_ for native animals. (worse)

5 It's **surprising** that bees are so dangerous.

I'm surprised that bees are so dangerous. (surprised that)

▶ WB p. 5; SB p. 11

More help **4** Safety advice for tourists

a) Complete the article with words from the box.

> bites • call • care • ~~climate~~ • cool • deadliest • down • heat • identify •
> light • protect • shade • shade • still • sting • use • water • wear

In hot weather

Parts of Australia have a very hot _climate_. If you suffer from _heat_ stress you should stay in the shade and use wet towels to _cool_ down. You should also drink a lot of water, and _call_ a doctor if you don't get better.

At the beach

Be careful if there are jellyfish[1] – bluebottles[2] are the _deadliest_. Swim with _care_ where there are strong currents[3]. And _protect_ yourself from the sun: use good suncream and _wear_ a hat and T-shirt.

In the outback

Take lots of _water_ with you – 10 litres per person per day. If your car breaks _down_, stay with it and use it for _shade_. If you get lost, _light_ a small fire and _use_ your whistle.

Snakes

If a snake _bites_ you, stay calm and _still_. Phone for an ambulance and try to _identify_ the snake so the doctor can give you the right anti-venom.

▶ WB p. 6; SB p. 13

---

[1] jellyfish _Qualle_   [2] bluebottle _Portugiesische Galeere (eine Qualle)_   [3] current _Strömung_

1 DIFF BANK

More help **11** **Saving baby kangaroos**

- Underline the verbs in the simple present (*what is / what happens*) in blue (5 examples).
- Underline the verbs in the simple past (*what happened*) in orange (6 examples).

This **is** Brolga. He **runs** a sanctuary¹ for baby kangaroos who **have** no mothers. He **started** in 2005. He **found** a dead kangaroo on the road. Its joey (the name for a baby kangaroo) **was** nearly dead, but Brolga **took** it home and **looked** after it. Now he **lives** with about 25 kangaroos in his sanctuary in central Australia. He **built** the sanctuary himself in 2009, and now he **helps** lots of joeys every year.

- Underline the verbs in the present perfect (*what has happened*) in red (1 example).
- Underline the verbs in the the going to-future (*what is going to happen*) in green (2 examples).

Soon, Brolga **is going to build** a kangaroo hospital. He **has already collected** quite a lot of money. "**It's going to be** a good year," says Brolga.

▶ WB p. 10; SB p. 17

More help **12** **Brolga's babies**

Put the verbs into the right tense: simple present or simple past.

Brolga *called* (call) the first joey he *saved* (save) 'Palau'. He still *gives* (give) all his joeys names. When Palau *was* (be) one year old, Brolga *let* (let) him go free in the outback. He *wants* (want) all kangaroos to live wild if they're healthy enough. Palau *went* (go) back to the outback after one year with Brolga.

Brolga *says* (say) that he *feels* (feel) like the kangaroos' mother! He *feeds* (feed) them and they *go* (go) everywhere with him – even to the supermarket! When they're small, they *stay* (stay) inside a bag, like their mother's pouch².

Australian and British TV companies recently *made* (make) programmes about Brolga, and lots of people *sent* (send) money. Brolga *hopes* (hope) he can continue his work for a long time.

▶ WB p. 10; SB p. 17

¹ sanctuary *Tierheim* ² pouch *Beutel*

seventy-two

DIFF BANK   1

More challenge 1 **Our school play**

a) Read the text and (circle) the words that show you what tenses to use.

b) Write the verbs in the correct tense:
simple present • simple past • present perfect • going to-future

(Every year), our school _does_ (do) a school play. The English teacher (usually) _organizes_ (organize) it, and (sometimes) the music teacher _helps_ (help). (Last year), we _did_ (do) a musical comedy. It _was_ (be) really funny. I've _been_ (be) in four plays (already), and I've _enjoyed_ (enjoy) every one. (Next summer), we're going to _do_ (do) a comedy, and I'm going to _play_ (play) the main character. I've _never played_ (never play) the main role (before). (At the moment) I'_m/am_ (be) quite nervous. But when we start (next April), I'm going to _practise_ (practise) a lot, so I think I'll be OK.

▶ WB p. 11; SB p. 17

More help 20 **What do you think?**

Give your opinion about the story. Answer in sentences.

- What do you think of the story and the characters?
- Would you like to read the book? Why / why not?
- Would you recommend[1] this book to a friend? Why / why not?
- How many stars would you give the story? (★ – ★ ★ ★ ★ ★)

Useful words and phrases:			
I think In my opinion	the story is the characters are	very … and quite …	good • exciting • interesting • funny • boring • too violent • glamorous • likeable • believable • enjoyable
I would I wouldn't	like to read the book recommend it	because	it's … I like / my friend likes … stories.
I would give this story … stars.			

▶ WB p. 13; SB p. 21

---

[1] recommend *empfehlen*

seventy-three 73

2 DIFF BANK

Unit 2

More help 3 Peer Pressure

b) SPEAKING Ask your partner the questions and say what you think too.
Do you agree with your partner?

Peer pressure: questionaire

1 What do you think? Is peer pressure a problem in school?
2 Can you think of one way of dealing with it?
3 Most teens want to fit in – true or false?
4 Do many people in your school year smoke cigarettes?

5 Is shoplifting a big issue in your area?
6 Do you and your friends agree on everything?
7 Do you feel comfortable with most things your friends do?

8 How much are you influenced by your friends?

> **Useful words and phrases:**
> I (don't) think so.
> Students / teachers could talk to…
> I think that's…
> Quite a lot of / a few / not many…
> I think smoking is…
> I'm not sure. / I (don't) think so.
> Some / most of the time. /
> No, not really. / No, never.
> For example…
> I'm influenced (quite) a lot. /
> I'm not influenced very much.

▶ WB p. 20; SB p. 33

More help 6 Peer pressure

a) Peer pressure is when you do things because other people do them. These things are often negative, but they can be positive. Put these examples in the right lists.

> taking drugs • volunteering • drinking alcohol • cyberbullying • doing sport • joining a club • shoplifting • eating healthy food • smoking cigarettes • not going to school • starting a new hobby

Negative peer pressure 👎	Positive peer pressure 👍
taking drugs	*volunteering*
drinking alcohol	*doing sport*
cyberbullying	*joining a club*
shoplifting	*eating healthy food*
smoking cigarettes	*starting a new hobby*
not going to school	

b) Compare with a partner. Can you write one more example on each list?

▶ WB p. 21; SB p. 34

74 seventy-four

DIFF BANK   2

More challenge 2 **Amy's next boyfriend?**
Amy phoned Charlie, a boy in her class last Friday. Read the conversation.
Then complete what Amy said to her friend one week later.

- Hi Charlie, it's Amy. Do you want to go out?
- Hi Amy. Er... I don't have time. I'm doing my homework.
- Well, maybe we can go out on Saturday afternoon.
- Uh, sorry, I can't because I'm going swimming.
- I have a good idea. I'll buy tickets for the disco on Saturday night!
- Oh. Um, well, I've already bought tickets. I'm taking Ellie to the disco.
- Oh. Er... OK... I'll see you at school on Monday.
- OK. Bye, Amy.

You know Charlie in our class? I phoned him last Friday...

I asked him _if he wanted to_ go out. He said that _he didn't have time. He was doing his_ homework. So I said that maybe _we could go out_ on Saturday afternoon. But he told me _he couldn't because he was going swimming_. So then I said that _I had_ a good idea. _I would buy_ tickets for the disco on Saturday night. Then he told me _that he had already bought_ tickets. He said that _he was taking Ellie_ to the disco. So I said that _I would see him_ at school on Monday. He isn't *that* nice, anyway!

▶ WB p. 25; SB p. 40

2 DIFF BANK

More help **13** **Word families**
b) Write these words in the table below.

- friendly   friend   friendship
- met   meet   meeting
- visitor   visit   visit   visited
- write   wrote   writer
- cleaned   clean   clean
- dance   danced   dancer   dance

person (noun)	thing (noun)	what people do (verb: simple pres.)	what someone did (verb: simple past)	describing (adjective)
writer	–	write	wrote	–
friend	friendship	–	–	friendly
–	meeting	meet	met	–
visitor	visit	visit	visited	–
–	–	clean	cleaned	clean
dancer	dance	dance	danced	–

▶ WB p. 26

More help **15** **What do these new words mean?**
Complete the sentences.

1 A **squatter** is someone who *lives in an empty house*.
  an • house • in • lives • empty

2 A **tramp** is someone *who doesn't have a home*.
  home • doesn't • who • a • have

3 To **hammer** on a door means *to knock very loudly*.
  to • loudly • very • knock

4 You can use a **candle** if *the lights in the house don't work*.
  the • work • house • in • don't • lights • the

5 When you close the **curtains**, people *can't look into the house*.
  house • look • the • can't • into

6 "I **have every right to** be here" means *"I'm allowed to be here"*.
  be • allowed • I'm • to • here

7 A **busybody** is *someone who is nosey*.
  who • nosey • someone • is

▶ WB p. 27; SB p. 43/p. 116

DIFF BANK

Unit 3

More help **5** What job is it?

a) Choose four jobs from the list below. Write the qualities you think are needed for each job – but don't write the name of the job. Write in your exercise book.

Example: *To be a _____ you need to be helpful and patient, and have good communication skills. You have to like young people. And you should be good at maths!*

> You can find useful words on p. 54 in your book and in Wordbank 2 on p. 143.

painter	doctor	mechanic
pilot	receptionist	florist
singer	soldier	bank manager
web designer	cook	baker

Useful words and phrases:

You need to be…
energetic • reliable • confident • helpful • patient • polite • fit • calm at all times • adventurous • brave • enthusiastic • friendly • hard-working • confident

You need to have…
a lot of courage • good communication skills • a lot of qualifications • a good voice • a good head for heights

You should be good at…
IT • cooking • working in a team • talking to people • finding solutions to problems

You have to like…
travelling • people • music

b) Your partner reads your descriptions and writes the names of the jobs.

Example: *To be a maths teacher you need to be…*

▶ WB p. 34; SB p. 55

3 DIFF BANK

More help **12** **Questions for your partner**

a) Write these questions.

1. `last Saturday? • do • What did • you`   *What did you do last Saturday?*
   Last Saturday I went... / I played... / I visited... / I went out with...

2. `at • sport? • good • Are you`   *Are you good at sport?*
   I'm very good... / I'm quite good... / I'm not very good ... / I'm terrible ... at sport.

3. `match? • been to a • football • Have you`   *Have you been to a football match?*
   I've been to... one football match / a few matches / lots of matches.

4. `watch • yesterday evening? • Did you • TV`   *Did you watch TV yesterday evening?*
   Yes, I did. I watched... (programme). / No, I didn't. I listened to... / went to... /

5. `your • Who is • singer? • favourite`   *Who is your favourite singer?*
   My favourite singer is...

6. `do you • How many • have? • video games`   *How many video games do you have?*
   I have about ... video games. / I have lots of / a few... video games. / I don't have any.

b) Ask your partner the questions. How many of your answers are the same?   ▶ WB p. 38; SB p. 61

DIFF BANK   4

More help **15** **Questions for a famous person**

a) Choose a famous person.
Complete the questions 1–10 that you'd like to ask him/her.

Questions	Answers
1 H*ow* old *are* you?	
2 *Are* you married?	
3 Wh*at* hobbies *do* you have?	
4 How many children *do* you *have*?	
5 What *are* their names?	
6 Wh*ere do* you live?	
7 Wh*at is* your job?	
8 *Do* you like your job?	
9 *Do* you *have* any pets?	
10 _____ ?	

b) Find the answers on the internet and complete the interview. ▸ WB p. 39; SB p. 61

More challenge 3 **Getting more information**

Make the follow-up questions.
Remember that in English the preposition usually comes at the end of a question.

1 I went to a friend's house yesterday. – Whose house *did you go to?*

2 I spent the evening with five friends. – Which friends *did you spend the evening with?*

3 Tina couldn't come because she had to look after someone. – Who *did she have to look after?*

4 We listened to some CDs. – Which CDs *did you listen to?*

5 And we talked about our teachers. – Which teachers *did you talk about?*

6 Then we made a get well soon card for someone in the class. – Who *did you make a get well soon card for?*

7 We looked at some websites. – Which websites *did you look at?*

8 And we sent emails to a few people. – Who *did you send emails to?*

▸ WB p. 39; SB p. 61

4 DIFF BANK

Unit 4

More help **3** Your phone and you

a) How many different things do you use your phone for?
Make a list in your exercise book, e.g.:
I use my phone to go online, video-chat…

Ideas:
go • take • surf • video-chat • make • play • look at • send • watch

the net • with friends • online • videos • phone calls • texts • photos • social media sites • games

b) Compare with a partner. Do you use your phone for the same things? What do you use it for *most*?

▶ WB p. 48; SB p. 77

More help **4** SPEAKING Technology then and now

Think about when your parents and teachers were young.
Discuss the answers to these questions with a partner.
Give your opinion too.

! Take turns to read the questions.

1 How do you think they listened to music?
2 How did they watch films?
3 How did they communicate with their friends?
4 How did they spend their free time?
5 Was this very different from today? How?
6 What were their mobile phones like?
7 Did they have smart phones?
8 What were their computers like?
9 Did they use the internet as much as you?
10 Did they have as much technology as you?

No way!   That's…   so weird / cool / uncool!
I can't imagine life without…
I think today's technology is better, because…
I think it was better then, because…
In the past you had to… / you couldn't…
Now we always …

▶ WB p. 48; SB p. 77

80 eighty

DIFF BANK   4

More help **9** **Manager of a band**

A new band are playing their first gig in two months' time.
What does their manager need to do?
Make a list of things to do in your exercise book.

> Make posters for the concert.
> Put up the posters. *(where? when?)*

! You can get ideas from the article on p. 50.

Ideas:

make	a website	to give to fans
put up	badges	of the best songs
make	videos	about the concert
put	a great logo	a week before the gig
start	a blog	with interesting information
design	posters	for T-shirts
get	the posters	of the band on a music site
	T-shirts	to sell at the concert
		with lots of photos
		in school, shop windows, in the library

▶ WB p. 51; SB p. 81

More challenge 4 **10** **Gemma's holiday**

Gemma is telling her friend about her terrible holiday.
Read the sentences and rewrite them using the third conditional.

Example: The plane was late so I had to wait ten hours at the airport.

1. It rained so we didn't go to the beach.
2. We didn't pay much for the holiday so the hotel wasn't nice.
3. The people weren't friendly so I didn't practice the language.
4. The food wasn't good, so I was hungry!
5. There were so many mice in my bedroom, I couldn't sleep.
6. There weren't any shops, so I didn't spend any money.

eighty-one **81**

4 DIFF BANK

Example:
If the plane hadn't been late, I wouldn't have had to wait ten hours at the airport.

1 If it hadn't rained, we would have gone to the beach.
2 If we had paid more for the holiday, the hotel would have been nicer.
3 If the people had been friendlier, I would have practiced my language.
4 If the food had been better, I wouldn't have been so hungry!
5 If there hadn't been so many mice in my bedroom, I would have slept more.
6 If there had been some shops, I would have spent some money!

▶ WB p. 52; SB p. 83

More help 17 **Everyone has a story.**
Choose Shark, Tommy or Tammy. Imagine his/her story.

Ideas:
How old was he/she when his/her parents died?
Where did the family live before?
What was their life like before?
What does this character think of the other people in the story?
What does he/she hope will happen in the future?

X was only…
Before the virus, the family lived in a big/small house/apartment in…
Their life was… easy/hard.
They were… quite/very rich/poor.
X loves/likes/doesn't like/is afraid of… because…
He/she hopes he/she… will be able to/will have/will get/will find/won't be…

▶ WB p. 55; SB p. 87

REVISION Lösungen 1–3

Unit 1

1 At a café

a) Complete this dialogue in a café.

Waiter   Hello, can I *help* you?
Customer   I'd like a cheese *sandwich* and a salad, *please*.
Waiter   *No* problem. And to drink?
Customer   A coffee and a *bottle* of water, please.
Waiter   Anything *else*?
Customer   No, that's *all*, thanks.
Waiter   *That's* sixteen dollars fifty, please.
Customer   *Here* you are.
Waiter   Thanks. *Have* a nice day.

b) *soup, tea, a bottle of orange juice, fish and chips, a chicken sandwich, chocolate cake, a scone, pizza, lemonade, cola, biscuits, burgers*

2 Healthy or junk?

(Sample answer) *I eat quite a lot of healthy food, but sometimes I eat junk food. For example, I often have chips and packets of crisps. I think I should probably eat more fruit and drink less cola.*

Unit 2

1 TV shows

a) 1 *science fiction film – E*   2 *cartoon – H*   3 *talk show – A*   4 *horror film – C*   5 *comedy – F*   6 *music programme – D*   7 *reality show – G*   8 *sports show – B*

3 A reality show

a) I saw a very *good* reality show. Twelve people were put on an island. They had to find food and water *quickly*, and it wasn't *easy*. They had to be *careful* because it's *dangerous* to drink dirty water. At first, the people argued *angrily* with each other. They made a fire but there was a *terrible* tropical storm and it rained *heavily* – and their fire went out. *Luckily*, things got better on the second day.

b) *(Lösungsvorschläge)* They were very *happy* because they found water. They put some in bottles and carried them back *carefully*, trying not to drop any. But it wasn't *clean* water so they had to boil it on the fire. On the fourth day, they saw a *small* rabbit in the *dark* forest. They crept up *quietly*, but one of the people saw a *big* snake and shouted *loudly* and the rabbit ran away. They had nothing to eat and were very *hungry*.

Unit 3

1 Your school

1 *c*   2 *a*   3 *f*   4 *d*   5 *g*   6 *e*   7 *b*

2 School subjects: good, better, best

For me, the *easiest* subject is art, because I'm quite *good* at drawing. I think the *hardest* subject is P.E. I'm very *bad* at all sports. I like languages, and I think that German is *easier* than French. Geography is OK, but it's *more difficult* than history. My *best* teacher is Mrs Simpson – she's great.

3 English lessons

1 *learn*   2 *read*   3 *work*   4 *listen*   5 *write*   6 *say*

4 REVISION Lösungen

Unit 4

1 A trip to our aunt and uncle's house

My brother and I went to stay in with *our* aunt and uncle and *their* four cats. My uncle took *me* and my brother to *his* favourite cafe and we had ice-creams. A friend of my uncle's saw *him* and he came over and sat with *us*. She's a singer and gave us tickets for *her* next concert! My aunt and uncle are really nice. We're going to stay with *them* again in the summer.

2 Asking for help

Complete the conversation with the missing words. You won't need all the words in the box.

Tourist	I *wonder* if you could help me. What *time* are the bus tours, please?
Assistant	Sure! They're *every* half hour from 10 am until 6 pm.
Tourist	How long does a tour *last*?
Assistant	*Nearly* two hours: about one hour fifty-five.
Tourist	*Thank* you. And how much does a tour *cost*?
Assistant	Fifty-two dollars *per* person.
Tourist	Thanks. I'd like three *tickets*, please.
Assistant	*Here* you are.
Tourist	Thanks for your *help*.
Assistant	You're *welcome*. Have a nice day.

PARTNER B

10 SPEAKING Talking about a picture

Talk to your partner for two minutes.

- What can you see in the picture?
- What is the boy doing on his phone?
- What things can you do on a mobile phone?
- What are the downsides of mobiles for teens?

> Say more than the minimum. Show how good your English is!
> There's a boy. ▸ There's a boy with short blonde hair. He looks about 16.

10 SPEAKING Role-plays

> Read all the things on the card before you start. Think about how to make complete sentences. Remember to say *please* and *thank you*.

1

You are Nathan's sister. Nathan is in the shower and can't answer his phone. You answer.
- shower
- Who is speaking?
- day? time?
- will tell Nathan
- bye

2

Phone your friend. Plan something together for the weekend.
- play badminton / weekend?
- free Saturday?
- free Sunday?
- sports centre / 2.30pm
- next to / rugby stadium / 12 or 26 bus

LANGUAGE FILE kompakt

Unit 1

NEW LF 10 Using tenses (Die Verwendung der Zeitformen) ▶ WB pp. 10–11

Du kannst die **wichtigsten Zeitformen des Verbs** im Englischen bilden. Manchmal werden sie anders **gebraucht** als im Deutschen. Das ist wichtig, wenn du **eigene Texte** schreibst.

simple present ▶ LF 1, p. 182

Cycling is Ben's favourite sport. He practises hard. He often wins races.
He doesn't like to lose them.

Mit dem **simple present** drückst du aus, was wiederholt oder nie geschieht. Du benutzt es, wenn du **Orte, Zustände, Gewohnheiten** und **Vorgänge/Abläufe** beschreibst und bei **Zusammenfassungen**. ▶ Skills file 8.4, p. 175.

present progressive (▶ LF 2, p. 183)

In this photo Ben is cyling down a street. Two boys are following him. A car is just coming from the right.

Mit dem **present progressive** drückst du aus, was **gerade geschieht.** Du benutzt es auch bei **Bildbeschreibungen**. ▶ Skills file 9, p. 179.

simple past (▶ LF 3, p. 183)

Mia met her friend Li in a cafe yesterday. They didn't eat a lot because it was a very hot day. But they had a big ice cream together.

Mit dem **simple past** sagst du, was **zu einer bestimmten Zeit** in der Vergangenheit geschah. Das **simple past** verwendest du in **Berichten** und beim **Erzählen**.

going to-future (▶ LF 8, p. 187)

What are Mia, Ben and Li going to do next Sunday?
They're going to go to a concert. (They've already got the tickets.)

Was jemand **in der Zukunft plant** oder **vorhat**, drückst du mit dem **going to-future** aus.

will-future (▶ LF 9, p. 187)

Ben: "I'm afraid I won't have time to come to your match, Mia. But I promise I'll be at your next match."

Mit dem **will-future** kannst du über die Zukunft sprechen, z.B. über **Vermutungen** und **Vorhersagen**.

Unit 2

NEW LF 20 Indirect speech (Indirekte Rede) ▶ WB pp. 24–25

Emily said (that) she liked Kai.
  Emily sagte, dass sie Kai mag/gut finden würde.

She told Kai her name was Emily and she hadn't been to this club before.
She was there for the first time.
  Sie sagte (zu) Kai, ihr Name sei/wäre Emily und sie wäre noch nie in diesem Club gewesen.
  Daher sei/wäre sie zum ersten Mal dort.

Steht das einleitende Verb im **simple past**, z.B. *said, told, added, answered, thought, explained*, verschiebt sich auch die Zeitform des Verbs der ursprünglichen Aussage meist ins **simple past** oder ins **past perfect** (letzteres häufiger in der Schriftsprache).
Dieses (Rück-)Verschieben in die Vergangenheit heißt auf Englisch **backshift** (of tenses).

Wenn **mehrere Aussagen bzw. Sätze in indirekter Rede** wiedergegeben werden, benötigst du nicht jedes Mal einen neuen Einleitungssatz.

NEW Indirect speech: questions (Indirekte Rede: Fragen) ▶ WB p. 25

Kai asked Emily, "Where do you live?"
→ Kai asked Emily where she lived.
  Kai fragte Emily, wo sie wohnt/wohne/wohnte.

He also wanted to know, "How did you get here?"

Bei der Wiedergabe von **Fragen in indirekter Rede** musst du die **gleichen Regeln** wie bei Aussagen beachten:
- **Personen** und **Pronomen ändern** sich je nachdem, wer spricht, denkt oder schreibt.

LANGUAGE FILE kompakt

→ He also wanted to know how she had got here.
    Er wollte auch wissen, wie sie hergekommen war.

Emily asked, "How often are you at this club?"

→ Emily asked how often he was at this club.
    Emily sagt: „Ich mag meinen neuen Freund Kai."

- Steht das **einleitende Verb** im *simple past* (z.B. *asked, wanted to know, wondered, thought*), verschiebt sich auch hier die Zeitform des Verbs, meist ins *simple past* oder **past perfect** (*backshift* of tenses).

! Wie im Deutschen steht **am Ende** einer indirekten Frage **kein Fragezeichen**, sondern ein **Punkt**.

Dan asked Emily, "Do you like our music?"

→ Dan asked Emily_ if she liked their music.
    Dan fragte Emily, ob sie die Musik seiner Band mochte.

Fragewörter werden übernommen, jedoch entspricht die Wortstellung im Nebensatz jetzt Aussagesätzen, vgl. ... *how often do/does/did he was ...* -> *subject – verb*: **S-V-(O)**

▶ LF 11, p. 188

He wanted to know, "Are you a good singer?"

→ He wanted to know if she was a good singer.
    ..., ob sie eine gute Sängern sei/wäre/sein würde.

Bei **Ja-/Nein-Fragen** wird (wie im Deutschen „ob") im Englischen *if* (oder *whether*) eingefügt. Auch hier gilt die **Wortstellung** von **Aussagesätzen**: **S-V-(O)**.

▶ LF 11, p. 188

He asked, "Can you come to the talent show?"

→ He asked if she could come to ....
    ... ob sie kommen könnte.

! Verwechsle *if* = **ob** in indirekten Fragen **nicht** mit *if* = *(falls) wenn*, was du aus *If*-Sätzen kennst.

▶ LF 22–24, pp. 196–198

NEW *Indirect speech: commands, requests, advice*
(Aufforderungen, Bitten, Ratschläge in indirekter Rede)

▶ WB p. 25

Dan told Kai, "Go and get something to drink for us."

→ Dan told Kai to go and get something to drink for us.
    Dan forderte Kai auf, etwas zu trinken für sie zu holen.

Aufforderungen, **Befehle** und **Ratschläge** werden in **Indirekter Rede** meist eingeleitet mit: *tell/told sb.* **to** *(do sth.)*

And he added, "Don't hurry!"

→ And he asked him not to hurry.
    Und er fügte hinzu, dass er sich nicht zu beeilen brauche/bräuchte.

Bei **Verboten** und **Verneinungen** wird vor dem Infinitiv mit *to* das **not** eingeschoben:
    tell/ told s.b. **not to** *(do s.th.)*
bzw.   *ask/ tasked s.b.* **not to** *(do s.th.)*

Kai told Emily, "You shouldn't listen to Dan."

→ Kai told Emily not to listen to Dan.

Kai said to Emily, "Please, don't believe my brother."

→ Kai asked Emily not to believe his brother.
    Kai bat Emily, seinem Bruder nicht zu glauben.

Bitten werden in **indirekter Rede** meist eingeleitet mit: *ask/asked sb.* **to** *(do sth.)*.

Unit 3

NEW **LF 12** Word order in questions
(Die Wortstellung in Fragen)

▶ WB pp. 38–39

Du erkennst eine Frage daran, dass hier **vor** dem **Subjekt** eine gebeugte **Verbform** steht.

Fragen mit *do/does* und *did*

Viele Fragen bildest du mit einer Form von *do*, einem Hilfsverb (*auxiliary*). Es „hilft" sozusagen dabei, dass die Wortstellung des zugrundeliegenden Aussagesatzes einfach erhalten bleiben kann. Vergleiche:

    Aussagesatz (**S**-**V**-**O**)   **Fragesatz** (**Hilfsverb**-**S**-**V**-**O**)
    Mia and Li play football.   ➡   Do Mia and Li play football? (*Ja-/Nein*-Frage)
                                    When do Mia and Li play football? (Frage mit Fragewort)

LANGUAGE FILE kompakt

Weitere Fragesätze:

question word	auxiliary do(es)/did	subject	(main) verb	
	Does	Ben	work	on Fridays?
	Did	he and Li	go	to the cinema?
What	does	Ben	watch	on TV?
Where	did	you	buy	that DVD?

Du beginnst die Frage mit (Fragewort +) *do/does/did*, dann folgt das **Subjekt** und dann das **Hauptverb** *(main verb)*.

! Keine **Umstellungen** von **Verb** und **Subjekt** wie im Deutschen:
Arbeitet Ben? → Does Ben work?

! Das Hauptverb steht **immer** in der **Grundform** (Infinitiv). Gebeugt (konjugiert) wird das Hilfsverb.

Fragen mit Formen von *be* und *have*

Wenn der Fragesatz eine Form von *be* oder *have* enthält, steht diese **vor** dem **Subjekt**.

question word	verb (forms of be / have)	subject	
	Is	Mia	Ben's sister?
	Are	Mia and Li	good friends?
	Have	you	been to school?
Where	were	you	last weekend?
What	are	Mia and Li	planning for Friday?

Ein **Fragesatz** mit *be* oder *have* wird gebildet, indem du die entsprechende Form, z.B. *is, was, were; have, has* **vor** das **Subjekt** stellst.

Fragewörter – *who, what, when, where, why, how, how long* – stehen am **Satzanfang**.

Unit 4

NEW LF 24 *If ...* (Conditional sentences type 3)
(Bedingungssätze Typ 3)   ▶ WB p. 52

Mit Bedingungssätzen Typ 3 **stellst du dir vor**, was **in der Vergangenheit** unter bestimmten Bedingungen hätte geschehen können: „**Was wäre gewesen, wenn ...**"

Nebensatz
If it had been warmer,
        Hauptsatz
        Li would have gone to the beach.
Wenn es wärmer gewesen wäre, wäre Li zum Strand gegangen. *(Es war aber nicht wärmer, und Li war nicht am Strand.)*

Hauptsatz
Li would have phoned Mia
        Nebensatz
        if she had had her new number.
Li hätte Mia (ja) angerufen, wenn sie deren neue Telefonnummer gehabt hätte. *(Aber sie kannte sie nicht oder hatte sie verlegt.)*

If Li had asked Mia's brother Ben, he could have helped her. ... hätte er ihr helfen können.

If she'd asked Ben, he'd have given her Mia's number. ... gefragt hätte, hätte er ihr ... gegeben.

Da die **Bedingung** im *if*-Satz **nicht erfüllt** ist, können über die **Folge** im **Hauptsatz** nur Vermutungen angestellt werden.

Im Deutschen verwendet man oft *wäre gewesen/ gegangen/...* oder *hätte gehabt/gegeben/...*

Die (nicht erfüllte) **Bedingung** steht im *if*-Satz. Das Verb steht im *past perfect* z.B. *had been, had had, had helped*.   ▶ LF 7, p. 186

Die (vermutete) **Folge** steht im **Hauptsatz**. Dort benutzt du *would/wouldn't* + *past participle* (3. Form).

! Auch hier steht kein Komma vor dem *if*-Teil.

Im **Hauptsatz** kann auch *could* + *past participle* stehen.

! Die **Kurzform** von *would* und von *would* ist *'d*:
he'd (= he would) have given.
she'd (= she had) asked.

eighty-seven **87**

QUELLENVERZEICHNIS

Titelbild

Shutterstock/Ralph Loesche

Illustrationen

David Norman, Meerbusch (S. 27; S. 82); **Dorina Tessmann**, Berlin (S. 11; S. 13; S. 18; S. 20; S. 22; S. 24; S. 25; S. 28 *oben li.*; S. 32; S. 33; S. 34; S. 41; S. 42; S. 44; S. 49; S. 52; S. 54; S. 61; S. 62; S. 75; S. 77; S. 81)

Bildquellen

action press, Hamburg (S. 10 *oben u. unten* (*u.* S. 72): AGB FILMS/SWNS.com; S. 12: REX FEATURES LTD.); Corbis, Düsseldorf (S. 6 *unten li.*: Minden Pictures/Norbert Wu; S. 8 *unten*: Sygma/Patrick Chauvel; S. 39 *unten*: Splash News; S. 56 *oben*: Ted Soqui; S. 68: Michael A. Keller; S. 84: Westend61/Uwe Umstätter); **dpa Picture Alliance**, Frankfurt/Main (S. 4 Jacqueline Freney: Actionplus; S. 23: empics); **Fotolia** (S. 28 *oben re., Mitte, unten*: weissdesign; S. 60 *unten*: Beboy; S. 65: Kablonk Micro); Glow Images, München (S. 27: Djavid Lundberg Akvari); **INTERFOTO**, München (S. 8 *oben*: NG Collection, *Mitte*: NG Collection); **LAIF**, Köln (S. 6 snake: Shannon Benson/VWPics/Redux); **mauritius images**, Mittenwald (S. 14 Mitte li.: Alamy/Reinhard Dirscherl; S. 35: Alamy/Nancy Honey; S. 56 *unten*: Alamy /Jeffrey Blackler; S. 64: Alamy/guy harrop); **Robert Campbell Jnr. Aboriginal History (Facts). Courtesy of the artist's Estate and Roslyn Oxley Gallery**, Sydney (S. 7); **Thomas Schulz**, Teupitz (S. 20); **Shutterstock** (S. 4 *oben*: Peter Zurek, Nr. 4 A: NAN SKYBLACK, Nr. 4 B: Filip Bjorkman, Nr. 4 C: BlankaB, Australia: skvoor; S. 6 (*u.* S. 71) bottle: Betacam-SP, jellyfish: sciencepics, *unten re.*: Space Monkey Pics, sunshine: Vibrant Image Studio; S. 9 *oben*: notkoo, *unten*: 1nana1; S. 11: Jason L. Price; S. 13 fuel: Teneresa; S. 14 *oben*: Richard Majlinder, Mitte *re.*: Brian Kinney, *unten*: Shane White; S. 19 oben: oliveromg, *unten*: Mattz90; S. 36: wellphoto; S. 38: Nejc Vesel; S. 39 *oben*: Brenda Carson; S. 46: Monkey Business Images; S. 47 *oben*: kostudio, *unten*: CREATISTA; S. 48: Eugene Sergeev; S. 50 *oben*: Nejron Photo, *unten*: totally out; S. 53 *li. u. re.*: Monkey Business Images; S. 55: Monkey Business Images; S. 58: Syda Productions; S. 60 *oben*: Leonard Zhukovsky; S. 63 *oben*: rolfik, *unten*: Mark Bridger; S. 71 fire: Pawelk)

eighty-eight